WRITING WITH PURPOSE AND PASSION

A WRITER'S GUIDE TO LANGUAGE AND LITERATURE

JEFF STALCUP

MIKE ROVASIO

Chabot College

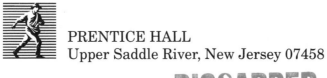

PRENTICE HALL
Upper Saddle River, New Jersey 07458

Library of Congress Cataloging-in-Publication Data

Stalcup, Jeff
    Writing with purpose and passion : a writer's guide to language
and literature / Jeff Stalcup, Mike Rovasio
       p.   cm.
    Includes index.
    ISBN 0-13-437609-9
    1. English language—Rhetoric. 2. English language—Grammar.
3. College readers. 4. Report writing. I. Rovasio, Mike
II. Title
PE1408.S667   1998
808'.0427—dc21   97-32576
                                              CIP

Acquisition Editor: Elizabeth Sugg
Editorial/production supervision, interior design,
   and electronic page makeup: Mary Araneo
Editorial Assistant: Emily Jones
Marketing Manager: Danny Hoyt
Director of Production and Manufacturing: Bruce Johnson
Managing Editor: Mary Carnis
Manufacturing Manager: Ed O'Dougherty
Cover Designer: Bruce Kenselaar
Cover Director: Jayne Conte

© 1998 Prentice-Hall, Inc.
Simon & Schuster/A Viacom Company
Upper Saddle River, New Jersey 07458

Printed in the United States of America

10 9 8 7 6 5 4 3 2 1

ISBN 0-13-437609-9

Prentice-Hall International (UK) Limited, London
Prentice-Hall of Australia Pty. Limited, Sydney
Prentice-Hall Canada Inc., Toronto
Prentice-Hall Hispanoamericana, S.A., Mexico
Prentice-Hall of India Private Limited, New Delhi
Prentice-Hall of Japan, Inc., Tokyo
Simon & Schuster Asia Pte. Ltd., Singapore
Editora Prentice-Hall do Brasil, Ltda., Rio de Janeiro

CONTENTS

PREFACE

Writing . . .

Of all the actions of which humans are capable, writing is perhaps the most significant. Writing is both personal and social; it provides us with a means of communicating with ourselves and others. Writing defines who we are and what we want. It describes how we think, feel, and dream, and it helps others to understand us in every way possible. Writing is analytical and fantastical. It is whatever we want it to be.

With Purpose . . .

Writers always write with a purpose, even if that purpose seems meaningless on the surface. This book attempts to instill in student writers the realization of *why* we write. Whether your writing is for a college course, a letter to a loved one, or simply a personal journal, there is always a reason why we write. This realization of purpose helps writers to focus the scope of the written words and to direct those words towards a particular goal or audience type. Such focus allows the writing to be better understood and appreciated by its readers.

And Passion . . .

Student writers often find it difficult to acquire passion, emotion, or feeling when writing. However, this dedication to writing is tied directly to purpose: If writers comprehend the reason for writing, they may find it easier to take an interest in the act of writing. So many students have expressed to us over the years how much better they felt about a piece of writing that dealt with a topic that they were "interested in." Both purpose and passion remove some of the fear that is typically associated with producing a piece of written work, and this book promotes these ideas throughout each chapter.

Writing with Purpose and Passion: A Writer's Guide to Language and Literature was written in response to the dire need for writing texts and materials at Heald Institute of Technology back in 1994. The vocational/technical curriculum seemed to ignore the need for an integrated approach to writing: As teachers we were unable to obtain texts that taught our students to read or to develop even the most basic essay forms. We decided to take matters into our own hands, and the result is this text.

This text combines an overview of the five most commonly used modes of rhetoric (description, narration, persuasion, comparison, and causal analysis) with a similar overview of the most common elements of grammar, punctuation, style, and usage. Added to this are many samples of student writing which demonstrate the rhetorical modes and principles of style and usage. It is this blend which makes this text the most complete book for students to improve their writing skills.

The writers would like to thank the following people, without whom none of this would have been possible: Mary Cullinan, Jacob Fuchs, Eileen Barrett, and all the faculty at California State University, Hayward who helped make this book possible. Thanks also goes out to Brad Burnett, graphic artist and designer, and thanks to all the students who proudly submitted their work to us for this text. The authors would especially like to thank our families—very special people who have supported us through the entire writing process.

Jeff Stalcup
Michael Rovasio

CHAPTER ONE

THE WRITING PROCESS

PREWRITING

Many writers would agree that starting an essay is perhaps the most difficult aspect of writing. You sit there, staring at a blank page or computer screen, and you cannot image where you will begin. At times the blank page may even seem to laugh at you, mocking you for your inability to mar its surface while the blank computer screen simply gives you a headache.

When students receive a writing assignment, they often feel overwhelmed. How long does it have to be, when is it due, and how do I start are often-asked questions. There is the feeling that a "perfect" paper must be handed in on the due date, giving the author only one chance at producing a piece of excellent writing. Students' perceptions that the writing process consists solely of sitting down and cranking out a draft for the date the paper is due causes debilitating stress for most students and overlooks the real process behind producing any piece of good writing.

Contrary to the popular belief, a piece of good writing does not suddenly come into existence. As with any skill, writing takes practice and uses a number of techniques specific to the process of writing. An extremely important technique to learn is how to generate ideas once you've been given a topic. This technique is known as prewriting.

Here are various prewriting techniques that you can use to help you generate ideas for writing. You may notice that many aspects of each technique overlap. Some methods are more involved than others. Choose whichever prewriting technique you feel the most comfortable with and the technique which best suits the needs of the given assignment.

Remember to be patient with yourself. Shakespeare was not a success overnight.

Researching

Researching a subject will help you understand the ideas surrounding the subject you've been asked to write about, which in turn will help you generate ideas in relation to what other authors have said on the subject. As with spoken conversation, it is much easier to come up with something meaningful to say when you know the subject of conversation. Research is an excellent way of learning the issues related to your writing assignment.

Don't be afraid to use your school's library or learning resource center. Most likely you will find plenty of information on the topic you must write about. Use the card catalog (or the electronic version of it) to find books which you can browse through. Use the periodicals and microfilm for articles related to your topic. If you have questions on how to find something, make the librarians earn their pay by asking them for help.

Once you've gathered material on the topic, begin skimming through it. Jot down any information that sparks your interest: phrases, words, titles, sentences. Soon you will see a pattern begin to develop and your ideas on the topic will begin to flow. Remember, if in the course of writing your assignment you decide to use a quotation from the sources you've gathered, be sure to give that source credit.

Brainstorming

Brainstorming can be done on your own or with other people. Many writers find brainstorming with their peers a useful prewriting technique. There is no right or wrong way to brainstorm, so long as you are able to create some material, even if it is only one or two minuscule ideas. The object here is quantity. Write down in the shortest form possible, even if it is only one word, any idea, however silly, that comes to mind. You can categorize your ideas or leave them strewn across the page as long as you put down as many ideas as possible.

Songwriters know that the more material you have, the greater the chances for a hit song. Working with friends can help you generate lots of ideas though you can just as easily brainstorm by yourself. Try to let go of stress and anxiety as you begin to write down your ideas. Reject nothing. Then after you exhaust all possible ideas, go back and pick out the ones that seem the best.

Some students run into a stumbling block during the brainstorming process because they mistake silly, crazy, weird, bad ideas for no ideas. Ideas that at first seem "stupid" can be reshaped and improved upon. In fact, that is what the writing process is all about. Even Virginia Woolf started with some bad ideas. But remember, the more ideas you have to choose from at the start, the easier it will be to choose worthwhile ideas to develop.

Clustering

People generally tend to develop ideas through association, and clustering is one way to group ideas of a similar nature so that recognizable patterns may emerge. In fact, you may be able to develop an entire essay through a grouping, or clustering, of your ideas. Consider this example:

> Let's say you've been asked to write a short narrative of a significant event in your life, but you're not sure which event to write about. First, write down the "significant event" in the center of your paper and circle it. Now list every possible event you can think of that might be considered significant, clustering them around your central topic. Are any of the events related? If so, connect them with a line, and then build from that. Soon you may see patterns begin to develop, patterns which may eventually lead you to a very focused topic for your essay. Figure 1-1 shows a student's clustering for this assignment.

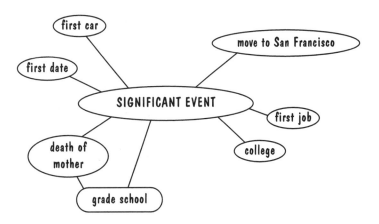

Figure 1–1   Clustering of a significant event.

Think of clustering as a detective unearthing clues for a case. In many instances, one clue will lead to another and another, until the final mystery—in this case, what to write about—is solved. You may be surprised by what you discover about yourself!

Freewriting

Sit down for a few minutes and just write freely. This is the essence of freewriting—literally, to write freely and without fear of error, organization, or clarity. Many teachers of writing agree that the best way to get started writing is simply to start writing, and this is exactly what freewriting enables a person to do. Freewriting can also generate ideas in a fashion similar to those of clustering.

Freewriting should be done for a period of no longer than 10 to 15 minutes, but you must write **constantly.** It is this constant contact between pen and paper that is the essence of freewriting, for not only are you thinking but also writing, and this process is often the most difficult obstacle in getting started.

Begin your writing by contemplating a major topic or idea. If, for example, you were writing about that same "significant event" from above, you might freewrite about whatever events that came into your head. Write down exactly what you are thinking; change topics as your mind changes topics; get down as much information as you can in 10 to 15 minutes.

Does this sound like regular writing to you? In a way it is, but the difference is that you never go back and edit or revise. The best part about freewriting is that you don't ever stop and contemplate what you've already written; you don't erase or change anything: you're always going forward. even if you can't think of what to write next, you must continue to write, regardless of the drivel that comes from your pen. Always keep writing! The following example, freewriting about a "significant event," gives a graphic demonstration of freewriting.

> significant event, huh? well i can think of a lot of significant events but I don't really know which to begin with. I suppose I could tell about the time I got my first job bussing tables at that cruddy old greasy spoon restaurant back in San Diego, and all the money I thought i was making at the time. Funny how i remember my crazy old boss more than anything, and how she seemed to take good care of me maybe she had a crush on me . . . can't think of anything to write write now write now write now write now, Robin was her name, and I think she did have a crush on me. I sued her for a reference to get an even better job waiting this time. That was a significant event.

Notice two things here: (1) the writer is totally unconcerned with errors in punctuation, spelling, etc. And why should he be? This is simply an exercise to generate ideas, so don't sweat it. The only one who will be reading it is you. Later, after you've milked it for all it's worth, you can throw it away; (2) the writer has lapsed from the topic occasionally, yet he has still continued to write. Proponents of freewriting insist that this is of paramount importance, for freewriting is as much a muscle-memory exercise as mental.

Listing

When ideas don't readily come to you, try making a list of any possible ideas related to the subject. It doesn't matter how good or bad the ideas are. Just get a list of some ideas going. Shoot for a list of at least ten items. You can always add or delete as you go.

Slowly read over your list until patterns begin to emerge. Don't be afraid if your list of ideas leads to other ideas you hadn't thought of in the beginning. Listing is a good tool to lead you from one idea to the next and to the next and so on. In fact, the ideas you finally decide to expand in your essay may not be the ones in your original list. At the same time, you may find relationships between your ideas that you hadn't known existed when you started listing.

Outlining

Making an outline is an excellent way to start the writing process because it helps to **organize** your ideas produced in the brainstorming portion. One of the most important aspects of creating a "good essay" is to organize your thoughts so that they may be presented clearly; nothing is more confusing for a reader than a jumbled bunch of information that seems to have no form or structure. A good outline can help a writer get a logical order figured out even before the first word is written. However, you should expect the shape of the outline to change as you shape your ideas.

To start your outline, you must first determine the length of your work. If your assignment asks for only a few pages (3–5) then two or three major topics may be sufficient; however, a longer assignment will certainly require more major topics and more corresponding subtopics. An outline, then, is simply a logical organization of major topics and subtopics.

One of the best ways to determine your major topics is to closely examine the assignment itself. Usually, the answer can be found in the wording of the question; at the very least you should be able to develop a **thesis statement** from it, and this in turn may lead to the development of the major topics. Consider the following sample assignment question. What might be a logical outline of the *major topics* for this assignment?

> Write a short personal narrative that recounts a "significant event" in your life. Describe the event as vividly as you can, and then try to determine how this event has affected you as the person you are today.

Look again at this example. The answer is in the question(s). Underline the parts of the assignment that give you writing directions or instructions. These directions will most often become your major topics, and your outline might look something like this:

> I.   Introduction
>   A.   Thesis
> II. Description of the event
> III. How the event has affected me
> IV. Conclusion

Taking Notes

Most instructors will help the class generate ideas for the writing assignment he or she has assigned. Take detailed notes during this time. Also take notes on the class discussions that evolve around the topic. When it is time to begin thinking about your topic, you can go back to your notes for ideas.

You'll often find your writing assignment is based on the ideas you've been reading about in your class. Many times the assigned essays are to serve as models for your own essays. Therefore, when class discussions center around the themes and ideas from your readings, take notes. Again, you can go back and review your notes, looking for ideas that spark your interest, ideas you can further develop in an essay.

Journal Writing

Keeping a record of your experiences and ideas can provide you with a myriad of topics for further expansion. Many writers go back to their journal entries when they need help with an assignment.

Journal writing also allows you to work on your writing style. If no one critiques your journal, you are completely free to experiment with various writing techniques that you can later use in an essay.

Your journal is also an excellent place to help you sort through your thoughts. Most people's natural thought process is confused, jumbled, and unclear. Journal writing allows you to reflect on your thought process as you write, without anyone looking over your shoulder.

Asking Questions

Imagine yourself a reporter for a newspaper or magazine. Begin asking questions of the topic you are supposed to write about. Who is this paper for—who will be my audience? Who or what is this essay about? What is my opinion on the topic? What is the topic? Where do the events take place? Why did something happen? When did it happen? How did it happen?

Asking the types of questions a reporter would ask is a useful way to analyze your assigned topic, drawing out the necessary information surrounding it. You may be surprised at how many angles from which you can approach a topic.

Discussion

This method of brainstorming may often be overlooked, but it has always worked well for our students. Discussion may enable those who are auditory learners to **hear** ideas rather than see them on paper. We recommend, however, that even if you choose to discuss ideas, you may want to have pen and paper handy so that you may note any ideas you encounter, unless you have an incredibly acute memory.

Discussion can be especially rewarding when used in conjunction with either clustering or freewriting, and we strongly recommend any combination of the three. Again, there is no right or wrong way to do this, but if the goal is to generate ideas, then we must get these ideas any way we can. Play around with our suggestions, or come up with some of your own.

DRAFTING AND REVISING

Once you have generated sufficient ideas, you are ready for the next step in the writing process: drafting and revising. Most instructors will allow you to write more than one draft of your essay so that you can hone your ideas and writing style. Even if your instructor does not give you credit or time for writing more than one draft, plan ahead. Leave yourself enough time to revise and proofread your essay.

We have found that three drafts of an essay help students produce a piece of writing that they and their instructors are satisfied with. The first draft allows the writer to develop ideas from the prewriting. The second draft allows the writer to work on better organizing and further expanding her or his ideas. For the third draft, basic grammatical errors and other typical mistakes can be corrected. Do not, however, feel limited to three drafts. Many writers revise their essays five, ten, twenty times or more.

Any experienced writer will testify that writing is really revising. Revising is not just correcting errors the instructor has pointed out. Rather, revision means you see what you have written in a different way. It may mean you need to add new examples, cut out wordiness, or rearrange the order of your ideas, among other things. At first, revising may seem a tedious task to you, but once you become used to "revisioning" your ideas, revising can be fun. The more you revise, the clearer your ideas become and the clearer your writing becomes. The more you revise, the better you will become at it, and the more satisfied you will become with your writing and the writing process.

You may now be asking yourself, "What about the actual writing of the draft?" "How do I start my first draft, and what do I need to put in it?" As with freewriting, there is no right or wrong way to go about writing an essay, but again, we have some suggestions for making the sailing a little smoother.

Identifying Major Topics

One of the most important aspects of creating a "good essay" is to organize your thoughts so that they may be presented clearly; nothing is more confusing for a reader than a jumbled bunch of information that seems to have no form or structure. The next step in the writing process, then, is to give your prewriting ideas a logical organization

After you have generated ideas through prewriting, there are many ways you could go about organizing them. First, you must be as familiar as possible with the ideas you have generated. Reread what you have written in your prewriting. As you read your ideas over and over, certain ideas will present themselves as important. Once you've identified the important ideas, you will want to organize them in what seems to you the most logical manner.

We have discovered a few methods that help us rearrange our ideas after prewriting.

1. List each idea on three by five cards or slips of paper that can be easily shuffled around. The point here is to arrange your cards or slips of paper so that one idea leads into the next, giving both ideas stronger support.
2. Cut your ideas out of the paper you've written them on and rearrange the pieces of paper.
3. Use the cut and paste feature in your word processing program.

Don't be afraid to try as many variations as possible. Eventually you will find a pattern that works the best. The major points will become obvious as well as supporting details and areas that need expansion. In essence, the above suggestions are ways of listing or outlining your ideas. If you've made a list of some kind or used the outlining method of prewriting, formalizing your list or outline is an excellent way to smoothly bridge the gap between prewriting and the first formal draft of your essay.

Thesis and Conclusion

The **thesis statement** is the controlling mechanism of your essay, and a strong thesis is essential for a well-organized piece of writing. The thesis states the writer's intentions, and it should also anticipate a focus or direction of the essay. Depending on the length of your assignment, the thesis may be a sentence or two, or it may be a number of paragraphs. Regardless of length, however, the thesis statement should usually be placed at the end of the **introduction.**

After you have developed a decent outline, your thesis will be easy to formulate because the thesis need only briefly explain what a reader may find in the pages that follow. A good thesis tells the reader *exactly* what is to come, in as specific a manner as possible. Keeping with the above topic/outline, consider the two following examples. One is more specific while the other is vague. See if you can determine which is more effective.

> In this essay I will relate to you a significant event from my life, and I will try to explain how it has affected me as a person.

> My first job was absolutely incredible, and it was certainly a very significant event in my life. Not only did it teach me responsibility at an early age, but it also taught me not to trust people, no matter what the circumstances, a lesson that I use even today in my everyday life.

Which seems to be more effective? Which seems to better explain not only the writer's intention, but also *specific* information about what the essay is about? It is not difficult to see why the second example is better. While the first seems to state the author's intention. It says virtually nothing specific about the material of the essay. The second example, on the other hand, explains with more concrete details ("first job," "responsibility," etc.) what the essay will cover. This is the essence of a strong thesis statement.

The Three Elements of a Good Thesis Statement

A good thesis statement should always have three very important elements which will clarify your topic and the main point of your essay:

1. **Intentions.** You should always start the thesis with a statement of your intentions as a writer. In other words, try to tell your reader *exactly* what your piece of writing will discuss:

> This essay will explore the civil rights philosophies of Dr. Martin Luther King, Jr. and Malcolm X.

2. **Method.** Explain to your reader *how* you will perform your intentions. This is a good place to describe your writing style (descriptive, narrative, persuasive, etc.) and/or titles of works that you may cite in your essay. Your reader will want to know how you will tackle your topic.

> The methods employed by these two men will be compared on the bases of their feelings about whites, their upbringing, and their educational background.

3. **Anticipate conclusions.** Try to state where you think your essay will go, where it will conclude. This will prepare your readers for what they are about to read. They will want to know, briefly, what your essay will discover, prove, or illustrate.

> Through an analysis of the speeches "I Have a Dream" and "The Ballot or the Bullet," I will show that King's dream was more practical and more successful in the civil rights movement.

A strong thesis statement, in many ways, is a slightly expanded outline of your essay. It should touch on all major topics of the writing itself so that the reader can get your main points at a glance.

4. **Conclusion.** The last major topic you should include in your essays is a conclusion. The conclusion is a summing up of the major ideas, and, if possible, a place for the writer to show how the intentions set forth in the thesis have been achieved. This is an opportunity for you to leave your reader with a positive thought, so it should not be wasted.

REWRITING THE ESSAY (REVISION)

Many student writers dread the act of revision, but it is as important as any of the other steps in the writing process. Ideally, writers would have an endless amount of time to write, rewrite, and rewrite some more, yet ironically a school calendar may not always allow for enough time to be spent on this precious step. Be sure to allow yourself **at least one-half of your time** for revision. You will constantly be going over an essay, making corrections, adding and deleting information. Think of your essay or story as a painting or a piece of sculptor's clay which must be molded slowly and artistically. Until the clay dries, the form may be shaped and changed in any number of fashions to suit the artist; you are a Michael-angelo, a Cellini. Remember, the ceiling of the Sistine Chapel was not painted in a day—not even a semester.

Now you are ready to learn some of the stylistic, mechanical, and rhetorical apparatus for creating good prose. In the pages that follow you will find detailed descriptions of how to write a variety of different types of essays and ways to improve your basic writing skills. Use this introductory chapter each time you begin a new essay, for it may help you to get started or to write each assigned paper.

And remember, writing should not be a hated, laborious process. Learn to relax. Play music if that pleases you, and enjoy your writing experiences! They are a journey into yourself.

REVIEW—GETTING STARTED

Answer the following questions using at least two or three complete sentences.

1. What is prewriting? Explain how prewriting can help you begin a writing assignment. Give three examples of types of prewriting.

2. Why is it important that you leave yourself enough time to write more than one draft of an essay? Why is revising a needed part of the writing process?

3. According to the chapter, what is an effective way to move from prewriting to drafting your essay?

4. Briefly describe the process of generating a thesis statement. Why is a strong thesis necessary in writing essays?

5. What kind of information should be placed in your conclusion?

6. Explain the analogy used to describe the written work as a piece of art. Why is *revision* important to the writing process?

WRITING ASSIGNMENTS

1.   Use the clustering technique to generate ideas for an essay.

2.   Freewrite for five minutes about an essay topic. Be sure to forget about spelling or punctuation as you freewrite.

3.   Using the process described in the chapter, generate a thesis statement for an essay assignment. Be specific.

CHAPTER TWO

THE PARTS OF SPEECH

INTRODUCTION

Why is it important to know and live the parts of speech?

1. **The parts of speech are the humus in the garden of the English language.** They sprout beautiful flowers, delicious fruits, and gangly green vines of words, and without them nothing would grow here. The parts of speech build sentences for us, and they allow us to enter into many different aspects of mechanics, usage, and so forth.
2. **We must learn the parts of speech so that we can have a working vocabulary of terms for our discipline of study.** In biology you must learn about ecosystems, genetics, and evolution; in electronics you learn about resistance and impedance; so in English we also have a vocabulary of specialized terminology that will allow you to understand how language works. You must know these terms so that an instructor can discuss your writing with you without having to say, for example, that "your whatchamacallit does not agree with your thingamajig."
3. **A good understanding of the parts of speech should necessarily lead to a better understanding of how the English language works.** The theory here is that if you understand the interworkings of the nuts and bolts, then you should also understand the machine itself. You should know how parts of speech work in sentences, and when and where to use each one. because this will prevent you from confusing certain parts of speech (as many neophytes do), your writing will be accepted and better understood.

THE PARTS OF SPEECH

Nouns

A noun is generally considered to describe a person, place, thing, or idea. Most people know this to be true, as this rule is drummed into many students' heads from a very early age.

> <u>Tom</u> left his <u>heart</u> at the <u>El Supremo Bar</u> and <u>Grill</u>.

However, nouns are used for a variety of purposes in the English language, many of which lead to other aspects of mechanics, style, and usage. Here are some other important reasons why we cherish the noun:

1. Plurality

A noun is the only kind of word that can be made plural, though not all nouns can be counted. Many people who are learning English as a second language try to make other parts of speech plural, but only nouns can be changed in this way (see the Appendix):

> Mom gave us one white <u>cat</u>, two black <u>cats</u>, and three calico <u>cats</u> for Christmas.

However, not all nouns can be counted this easily. What about *love, intelligence,* or *insanity?* Some nouns are so abstract that you simply cannot count them up. These are known as non-count nouns.

2. Possessive

Nouns may also be used in pairs to show possession. When one noun belongs to or is related to another noun, the apostrophe and -s ending are used to show the possessive case.

> Come hear Uncle <u>John's</u> band, by the <u>river's</u> side.
> —The Grateful Dead

3. Subjects of Sentences

Nouns, along with pronouns, are always the subjects of sentences. You must have a noun or pronoun to make a sentence complete. This is discussed in greater detail in Chapter 4.

4. Capitalization

When a noun names a specific person, place, or thing, it is called a proper noun. A person's name (Henry Weinhard) or the name of a certain place (Yoncalla, Oregon) are always capitalized (see the Appendix for specific rules on capitalization).

Pronouns

Pronouns are usually defined as substitutes for nouns. A pronoun can be used to rename another noun used in the same sentence (known as the antecedent), or pronouns may stand alone as the subject of a sentence. There are approximately one hundred pronouns in the English language, and they fall into seven distinct categories.

1. Personal Pronouns

A personal pronoun renames a particular person or thing in a sentence. These pronouns may be further subdivided into two categories: subjective (when used as the subject of a sentence) and objective (when the pronoun is an object). Many times these pronouns are confused with one another, so it is good to get the two forms straight:

> **Subjective:** I, you, he, she, it, we, they
>
> **Objective:**   me, you, him, her, us, them
>
> <u>I</u> gave all of my candy to <u>him</u>, for a price.
> SUBJECT   OBJECT

2. Possessive Pronouns

These pronouns are used to indicate ownership. In the English language, possession can take many forms, and possessive pronouns are one way to show that relationship. See the Appendix for more information about possessive situations. The possessive pronouns take one of two forms, singular or plural:

> **Singular:** my, mine, yours, his, hers, its
>
> **Plural:**   ours, yours, theirs
>
> <u>My</u> motocross was faster than <u>theirs</u>.
> SINGULAR   PLURAL

3. Demonstrative Pronouns

A demonstrative pronoun indicates or points to a particular noun. We use the term "points to" because this is often the way people use them in everyday speech:

Demonstrative Pronouns: this, that, these, those

These cans are defective!

—Steve Martin, *The Jerk*

4. Relative Pronouns

These pronouns introduce subordinate or non-restrictive clauses that function as adjectives. The appositive and adjective clause are used to modify nouns in a sentence. Relative pronouns usually rename an antecedent noun:

Relative Pronouns: who, whom, which, whose, that, what

The tree, which blooms every year, is home to tiny elves.
(MODIFIES "THE TREE")

Who, whom, and *whose* usually refer to people or animals. *Which* usually refers to things. *That* can be used for either.

5. Interrogative Pronouns

An interrogative pronoun is used to begin a question. These pronouns (with the exception of *that*) are identical to the relative pronouns, but they are always followed by a phrase that ends with a question mark.

Interrogative Pronouns: who, whom, whose, which, what

What would you say if I sang out of tune?

—The Beatles

6. Indefinite Pronouns

These pronouns are aptly named, and they can be easily remembered because they refer to non-specific, or indefinite, persons or things. When a writer is not exactly sure how much, how many, or which particular nouns are involved, he or she can use the indefinite pronoun. Below are listed the most common indefinite pronouns, and each is marked as either singular (s) or plural (p). Often, writers will confuse singular and plural forms simply due to the indefinite nature of the beast. You should try to remember the most common indefinite pronoun forms:

Indefinite Pronouns

all (p)	anything (s)	everyone (s)	nobody (s)
any (s)	both (p)	everything (s)	none (s)
some (p)	each (s)	neither (s)	someone (s)
anybody (s)	either (s)	nothing (s)	something (s)
anyone (s)	everybody (s)	many (p)	somebody (s)

7. Reflexive Pronouns

Reflexive pronouns tend to emphasize or reflect another noun or pronoun. In the case of reflection, the subject (which performs the action of the verb) also receives the same action as the direct object. Reflexive pronouns may also be singular or plural:

Singular: myself, herself, himself, itself, yourself

Plural: ourselves, yourselves, themselves

Billy pinched <u>himself</u> to make sure he wasn't dreaming.

This pronoun section should serve as your reference guide. Though you may never be tested on pronoun forms *per se,* you should be as familiar with these parts of speech as possible. Pronouns are versatile tools and should be used correctly, judiciously, and responsibly.

Verbs

A verb is a word (or words) that expresses action, and every complete sentence must contain a verb. Verbs are the most complex parts of speech. If they were grapes they would produce a rich, full-bodied Bordeaux that you could store in your wine cellar for years. Just as the grape is the heart of a good wine, the verb is the heart of every English sentence.

To make your writing lively and accurate, there are three features of the verb you should familiarize yourself with: (1) **active** constructions, (2) **passive** constructions, and (3) verb **tense.**

1. Active Constructions

When a verb is an active verb, it is the word in the sentence that describes the action the subject does or did.

> Lola <u>smiled</u> and <u>took</u> me by the hand.
>
> —The Kinks

Smiled and *took* are the actions performed by Lola.

Most of the time the action being performed is obvious. At other times, the verb may be more abstract, causing you to question the action.

> I <u>have</u> a cold.

> She <u>thought</u> about the topic.

> We <u>love</u> our dog.

In the context of the above sentences, *having, thinking,* and *loving* are actions performed by the subjects. Thus, the sentences are active verb constructions.

Because active verb constructions show that the subject has committed an action, active constructions are livelier to read and present a sense of immediacy to the reader. Unless you are doing scientific or technical writing, you should always favor active verb constructions over passive verb constructions. An essay written in passive voice will eventually bore your reader.

2. Linking Verbs and Passive Verb Construction

Every sentence in English must contain a main verb. Action verbs fulfill this requirement. There are, however, other verb constructions that fulfill this requirement without requiring the subject to be the doer of the action.

Linking Verbs   Linking verbs are verbs that link the subject of the sentence to the subject complement. A subject complement is simply a word or phrase that helps describe or define the condition of the subject.

> **Incorrect:**   He sick.
>
> **Correct:**   He <u>feels</u> sick.

Correct:	He <u>is</u> sick.
Correct:	He <u>seems</u> sick.
Correct:	He <u>sounds</u> sick.
Correct:	He <u>appears</u> sick.

Incorrect:	The food bad.
Correct:	The food <u>tastes</u> bad.
Correct:	The food <u>smells</u> bad.
Correct:	The food <u>looks</u> bad.

In the above sentences, the verbs used simply link the subject to the information after the verb. There is no action taking place in the above sentences, but because English requires that every sentence has a verb, a linking verb must be used. There are times when linking verb sentence constructions are unavoidable, but when there is a choice, favor active verb constructions.

Passive Verb Constructions   To appear objective, scientists and technicians often rely on passive verb constructions. While in an active sentence the subject is doing the action and in a linking verb sentence there is no action, in a passive sentence the subject is acted upon by someone or something.

The frequency counter <u>is used</u> by technicians everywhere.

The experiment <u>was conducted</u> under extreme conditions.

In a passive sentence, the doer of the action appears in a prepositional phrase that begins with the preposition **by,** usually appearing at the end of the sentence. However, there are times when the "by" phrase is eliminated, and the doer of the action is implied (see the second example above).

3. Verb Tense

There is a multitude of verb tenses which serve a variety of purposes, all of which express when an action takes place. To help create different moments of time, helping verbs can be joined with simple action verb forms. There are a limited number of helping verbs in the English language. They are listed below.

Table 2-1   Verb Usage

	Past	Present	Future
Simple (one verb only)	• Used for actions begun and completed entirely in the past	• Used for habitual actions • Used for actions occurring at the time of speaking or writing • Used to state facts or general truths (generalities) • Used to express future action that will occur in a specific time • Used when writing about action in literature	• Used for action that will occur in the future • Used for facts that are predictable, given certain causes
Perfect (*to have* + past participle)	• Used for action completed before another past action • Used for an action completed at some specific past time	• Used for actions begun in the past and continuing in the present • Used for action begun in the past and finished at the time of speaking or writing	• Used for actions that will have been completed before or by a certain time
Progressive (*to be* + present participle)	• Used to express continual action in the past	• Used for actions that are currently in progress at the time of speaking or writing • Used for future actions that will occur at a specific time	• Used to express future actions that will continue progressively

The nine most commonly used ways of expressing different aspects of time, depending upon the situation, are displayed in Table 2–1.

Helping Verbs   Certain types of helping verbs, the **modals,** are never used as main verbs. They must be used **with** main verbs. The modals are:

Verb Modals

can	should	may
will	could	might
shall	would	must

Other helping verbs, such as *be, do,* and *have,* can be used as main verbs in a sentence. These forms tend to be somewhat irregular, so their forms are listed:

Infinitive Form

TO BE:	am, are, is, was, were, being, been, will be
TO DO:	do, does, did, doing, done, will do
TO HAVE:	have, has, had, having, will, have

Adjectives

An adjective is used to modify, or describe, a noun or a pronoun. Writers use adjectives to clarify or specify such things as color, size, shape, disposition, or type. Adjectives also allow writers to answer such questions as "How many?" "Which one?" or "What kind?"

Adjectives may also cause some writers a number of headaches, for sometimes adjectives are easily confused with other parts of speech. Both nouns and verbs may be made into adjectives simply by adding a suffix. This similarity is what causes the confusion. Don't be frustrated! See how easily a word can assume the shape of another part of speech:

love (noun) + **-ly**	=	**lovely** (adjective)
hate (noun or verb) + **-ed**	=	**hated** (adjective)

Parts of speech may be distinguishable by only a letter or two, or in some cases they are identical words. This is one of the strongest arguments for studying not only the parts of speech, but the contexts of those parts of speech as well. You must know context so that you do not confuse parts of speech in your writing.

PRACTICE

Modify the following nouns with an appropriate adjective form. Use a dictionary if needed. Be sure to write in complete sentences or paragraphs.

The **<u>arrogant</u>** seal trainer was knocked over by his **<u>angry</u>** pupil.

1. whale
2. child
3. water
4. glass
5. popcorn vendor
6. tourist
7. aquarium
8. sea otter
9. waves
10. ticket booth

Adverbs

Like adjectives, adverbs are used to modify or describe. However, unlike adjectives, which describe only nouns, adverbs modify three other speech parts—verbs, adjectives, or other adverbs.

Adverbs that modify verbs.   These adverbs will tell a reader how an action was performed, or when, why, where, or to what degree. An adverb that modifies a verb is movable—it can be placed either before or after the verb:

The pitcher threw the ball <u>wickedly</u> to home plate.

or

The pitcher <u>wickedly</u> threw the ball to home plate.

Another characteristic of adverbs that modify verbs is that they often are derivatives of adjectives, but with an -ly ending:

wicked (adjective)   ➔   **wickedly** (adverb)

Adverbs that modify adjectives or other adverbs.   These adverbs, unlike those that modify only verbs, are used to show a degree of intensity, and they may not be placed before or after the verb. Usually, these adverbs occur before the word being modified:

The dog was bad.   ➔   **The dog was <u>very</u> bad.**

but not

The dog was bad very.

Adverbs are also versatile tools, especially in descriptive writing. When used appropriately, and with effective adjectives, these parts of speech can help a writer add incredible clarity to an action or a scene. Adverbs are your friends; get to know them!

Prepositions

A preposition is used to express the spatial relationship between two or more nouns. Usually, prepositions are used as the first word of a prepositional phrase—a subordinate word group that may function as an adjective or adverb in a sentence.

> Last season, the A's finished <u>in</u> the cellar, some twenty games <u>below</u> the first place White Sox.

There are approximately 65 prepositions that are commonly used, most of which you will find in the table below.

Common Prepositions

about	below	for	opposite
above	beside	from	out
across	between	in	outside
after	beyond	inside	over
against	but	into	past
along	by	like	plus
among	concerning	near	than
around	considering	next	throughout
as	despite	of	to
at	down	off	underneath
before	during	on	upon
behind	except	onto	with

Many students of writing have trouble with prepositions because certain prepositions go with certain nouns or verbs. For example, we always throw *to* somebody, and we always refrain *from* doing something. Students are encouraged to listen to spoken and to read written prepositional phrases so that they may adopt these various usages.

> The pitcher tips his cap and throws to first base. This is to prevent the runner *from* stealing second base.

Conjunctions

A conjunction is an extremely helpful part of speech because it can directly affect the construction of your sentences. By using conjunctions effectively, you will see a noticeable improvement in your ability to write longer, more complex sentences. Think of conjunctions as the glue that binds words, clauses, and phrases. Attach your word groups with them; add other word groups to make the compound sentence, the complex sentence, and the compound-complex sentence.

> Bring ten balls <u>and</u> two bats, <u>or</u> don't come at all.

Conjunctions may be classified into four major categories:

- Coordinating conjunctions
- Subordinating conjunctions
- Correlative conjunctions
- Conjunctive adverbs

Common Conjunctions

Coordinating Conjunctions	Subordinating Conjunctions	Correlative Conjunctions	Conjunctive Adverbs
for	as	either...or	however
and	because	neither...nor	consequently
nor	if	both...and	moreover
but	since		thus
or	when		therefore
yet	while		furthermore
so	(see p. 53 for more)		

Interjections

An interjection is used primarily in speech or written dialogue. It is a one or two-word expression, accentuated with an exclamation point (!). It shows emotion, surprise, or anger.

> Hey! Stop! That's my car! They're stealing my car!
> —Gene Wilder, *Bonnie and Clyde*

PRACTICE

1. Demonstrate your knowledge of parts of speech by writing a sentence using the part indicated. Underline the part of speech you are using.

a. noun   f. adjective
b. proper noun   g. adverb
c. pronoun   h. conjunction
d. verb   i. preposition
e. helping verb   j. interjection

2. Go to the reading at the end of any of the writing style chapters. Identify each of the parts of speech listed above at least once as they occur in the reading assignment. Then, after you have made a positive ID, give a one or two sentence explanation of how you knew which part of speech it was, based on context. This will help you see how different parts of speech work in actual essays.

3. Change the following words to the parts of speech that are indicated in the parenthesis. Then use them in complete sentences. Use a dictionary if necessary.

a. quiet [adverb]   f. run [adjective]
b. noisy [noun]   g. smoothly [noun]
c. bored [adjective]   h. create [adverb]
d. elected [verb]   i. departed [verb]
e. serve [noun]   j. establish [adjective]

NAME:_____

WRITING ASSIGNMENT

Edit a draft for errors in the parts of speech. Make sure that each word that you've used is doing exactly what it should be.

Edit the following paragraph for errors of the parts of speech. Get into the habit of good proofreading! Use a dictionary for reference.

When I visited Walden Pond, I was somewhat amazed at the scenic that greeted me there. Thoreau had described it in his well-read work *Walden*, and I expectedly something much more peaceful and serenity. There at the shore I saw literal hundreds of people swimming, running around, screaming, drinking cans of soda, eating, and so forth. It was not at all what I'd excepted; I did not feel good at all. Later, though, I discovered the essential of Walden Pond when I hiked around to the backside. There I found the beautiful described by Thoreau.

CHAPTER THREE

DESCRIPTIVE WRITING

DESCRIPTION

This form of writing is very important to learn because as human beings, much of what we understand comes to us through our sensory perceptions. Description allows a writer to communicate sensual images through his or her words, and it enables a reader to really see, hear, smell, or feel exactly what the writer has already seen, heard, smelled, or felt. A good description opens our eyes to the beautiful colors of a sunset; it allows us to envision the appearance of a particular person (or fictional character); it brings us the smell of fragrant flowers; it chills us with a winter storm or warms us with a summer's breeze. Descriptive writing does all of this and more for a reader, and the best way to "give life" to your writing is to understand how good descriptions are made. Practice, of course, will also be necessary to hone your descriptive skills.

Appealing to the Senses

One of the easiest ways to create effective descriptions is to use sensual imagery. Because human beings receive information about their surrounding environment through the five senses—sight, sound, touch, taste, and smell—a good description will incorporate as many sensual images as possible. When you are writing a description, try to stimulate as many of these senses as you can, for when one or more of our senses are dull, we do not receive as clear an understanding than we would if they are all working properly.

Imagine if you suddenly found yourself blind. Without this important sense, you would not be able to see anything. Now close your eyes and describe to yourself all of the information that the other four senses are receiving. Perhaps you hear other students shifting in their desks around you; you may feel the texture of your desk, pen, or the temperature in the room; and you may smell any number of scents; however, without your sense of sight, your perception of what is around you is not as complete, and if you were to write a description without any visual images, it too would be incomplete.

When you write a description of sensual images, follow these simple rules:

1. Appeal to the most "important" senses first.

Obviously, sight is most important to human beings. We see many colors, perceive depth (3-dimensional), and have the ability to make many types of judgments on sight alone. Your description, in order to be effective, should include visual images whenever possible. Consider this example:

> The sequoia was an immense tree, towering 300 feet over the forest floor. The base was so thick that I could spread my arms out wide and still not reach a curve in the trunk. Large black ants crawled everywhere over the red bark, creating a contrast of color. The needles were bright green and serrated, like the blade of a bread knife.

Notice how this writer has used specific visual images to describe the tree: height (300 feet); width (greater than both arms fully extended); color (red and bright green); shape (like the blade of a bread knife). All of these descriptive elements help a reader to "picture" the tree in their minds, and since sight is so important to humans as a sense, appealing to it will often have positive results in terms of a written description.

Remember, however, that it may not always be prudent to rely heavily on visual description, especially in cases where sight may be limited. If, for example, you are describing a night hike through the woods, the absence of light would make things difficult to see, so you might want to de-emphasize visual images and focus on other senses. Consider this description:

> We walked on, through the darkened forest. We could see nothing, for it was dark. The shadows were just a bit more black than the night itself. Up above the tree canopy we could see the sky, just slightly lighter in black than the rest of the forest. I could not see my companions in front of me because it was so dark...

How effective is visual description in this example? Not very effective at all, is it? As a writer, you must decide which senses will provide the best possible details about the surroundings you are trying to describe. In the example above, the writer might have described the sounds of the forest, or the feelings associated with not being able to see, rather than constantly restating the fact that it was dark and therefore difficult to see.

Similarly, if you are describing a rock concert from the farthest seats away, it may be a better idea to describe the sound of the music rather than the ant-sized musicians on the stage below:

> The Grateful Dead was really rocking the place. Even though I was seated against the back wall of the arena, the sound quality was incredible. During the song "Space," I could feel the rumble of the double drum kit all around me, like thunder from a fierce winter storm. The electronic effects pierced the quiet crowd like arrows of lightning, sudden and intense. There were squeals of laughter from the crowd with each new sound, and though the musicians were like ants on the stage, their beautiful sounds reached our ears just fine.

As the writer, you must always make judgment calls like these. The bottom line, however, is that you should try to emphasize that sense that is most prominent in the description, and that decision will be based on exactly what is being described.

2. Appeal only to senses that are relevant.

When you are writing a description, you should try to include as much sensual imagery as possible, but do not feel that you have to stimulate **all five** of your reader's senses. In fact, a description may be ruined by overkill, especially if you would not normally associate a particular sense with the object you are describing.

For example, if you were describing an orange, you could describe its color, size, and shape (visual imagery), its smell, its taste, and the texture of the skin. However, you would be hard pressed to describe the "sound" of an orange. What, if any, relevance does the sound of an orange (is there such a thing?) have to your perception of it?

Similarly, if you were describing a baseball, you might describe its size, shape, color (visual), texture, hardness, and smell, and you might even be able to describe the sound a baseball makes when it comes into contact with a bat or glove. But it would not be wise to stick the baseball in your mouth to see what it tastes like. Firstly, it could be dangerous (due to germs or the inability to remove the ball once it's in place), and secondly, the "taste" of a baseball has almost no relevancy to our understanding of what it is.

The thing to remember here is this: choose your sensual imagery judiciously. Do not feel that you have to use all five senses to create a perfect description. Before you begin to write, sit down and decide which senses you should address and why. Usually it will be painfully obvious which to describe.

3. Write, don't list.

One pitfall that beginning writers tend to encounter is the sensual descriptive list. They depart from organizing ideas and begin instead to make lists of what the senses receive. Consider this example:

> The baseball is round, hard, and covered with a white leather skin. It feels very smooth to the touch, but it is very hard too. It smells like leather, and it has many red stitches that criss-cross its body. It makes a distinctive sound when struck by a bat or caught in a glove.

While this is perhaps an accurate description of a baseball, it is indeed a very boring one. The writer has reduced the baseball to a simple set of words that have little or no flair, and a reader may find it difficult to have any interest whatsoever in this object.

4. Use simile.

We recommend that writers try to bring their object to life. Give each sensual image its own paragraph, and go into detail about how people may perceive that image. One way that writers bring their descriptions to life is by the use of a comparison, also known as **simile.**

A simile is a comparison between two objects using the words "like" or "as." Similes are quite common in our everyday language, as described by these examples:

> The bank robber was sly <u>like</u> a fox.

> The baby's skin was as smooth <u>as</u> silk.

The comparison is an excellent way to bring life to the object, for people tend to associate things or ideas instinctively, and a well-chosen simile can bring an immediacy to the object. Most people know that foxes are sly and that silk is smooth, so the comparison stimulates more than just our five physical senses. Consider this simile used by the author Annie Dillard in her description of a baseball:

A baseball is smooth, <u>like</u> skin stretched tightly over bone.

All a reader must do to appreciate this description is to look at his or her own limbs, to stretch the skin tightly over a bone, and then that reader will "get" the simile.

5. Describe function as well as physical attributes.

Many objects of description can be explained through cerebral process (much in the way a simile stimulates our minds), and one very good way to do this is to describe how something works or what it does. For example, if we return to our description of a baseball, we might spend a paragraph on the seams alone, for not only do they have a physical appearance but a practical function as well:

There are approximately 100 stitches on a baseball. They are colored red, which creates a sharp contrast from the white leather skin of the ball. The stitches form a kind of elongated circle around the ball, and they have two particularly important functions: (1) to hold the leather skin in place, and (2) to enable a pitcher to put any number of spins on the ball that will make it more difficult for a batter to hit.

This writer then went on to demonstrate various pitches that a pitcher could throw by gripping the stitches in different ways. This explanation of function brings a great deal of importance to a seemingly insignificant part of the baseball; moreover, a person who is unfamiliar with the game of baseball may also learn something that he or she did not previously know. In this manner the writer has accomplished two things: a good description of the baseball, and a simple explanation about one aspect of the game itself. This is what is meant by "bringing life" to a description, and if you are able to accomplish more than simple sensual images, your description becomes much more effective as a piece of writing.

The ability to write a good description is not something that can be attained overnight; it takes practice not only in writing, but also in observing objects in their natural surroundings. Take the time to really get to know whatever it is you are describing. Think long and hard about it first, and get a good set of sensual images in your own mind before you start to write. Think about sight, sound, touch, taste, and smell. Think about other objects that you may compare your object with, or consider the function or action that it performs. A good understanding of all of these attributes will enable you to write a clear, effective description of anything that you wish to describe.

Answer the following questions with two to three complete sentences.

1. According to the chapter, what is the purpose of descriptive writing? Give an example or two of things that can be described in writing.

2. What is meant by the phrase "appealing to the senses?" Give an example of a descriptive sentence that appeals to one of the five senses.

3. According to the chapter, why is it important to discriminate when appealing to the senses? In other words, why should you not always describe ALL sensual imagery?

4. What is simile? How is it used in descriptive writing? Give an example.

5. Why is it sometimes helpful to describe an object's function? Briefly explain how this might add to the quality of a written description.

6. Try to brainstorm some ideas you may have for a descriptive essay of a person or a place.

VOCABULARY—DESCRIPTION

Words:

1. fragrant

2. sensual

3. texture

4. simile

5. metaphor

6. strewn

7. anticlimactic

8. gradient

9. arid

10. imagery

1. Look up the preceding words in your dictionary. Identify the most meaningful definition and the PART OF SPEECH. Now write the words in sentences to show their meanings.

2. Using your dictionary, work with a small group to write a two to three paragraph description or story. Try to use all of the vocabulary words from the preceding list in your sentences. Make sure that each sentence follows logically from the previous person's.

3. Define the words from above by their context from the readings. Are there any other uses or meanings for these words?

WRITING ASSIGNMENTS

1. Choose an object in the room. Describe only its physical attributes that pertain to **sight.** Consider color, size, shape, etc. Try to "paint a picture with words."

2. Find an object in the room and describe it in terms of its physical appearance (sight) **and** its apparent function. What does the object look like, and what does it do?

3. Study the following adjectives. Try to create similes by comparing them with other things or ideas that you associate with each adjective.

a. hungry   f. difficult
b. dirty   g. fast
c. ugly   h. slow
d. beautiful   i. furry
e. simple   j. weak

4. Recall your favorite place. Go there and sit or visit it in your mind. Describe this place for your reader using sensual imagery, simile, metaphor, etc.

5. Describe an individual human (or pet) who has had a profound impact on your life. Introduce this person to your reader.

READING REVIEW—DESCRIPTION

Read the following writing samples, then answer the questions that follow with two to three complete sentences.

1. Find two examples where one of the authors has used sensual imagery to describe a person or a place. What senses have been stimulated in you as a reader?

2. Locate and describe two examples of simile in any of your readings.

3. Outline one of the essays in your assigned reading. How has the author organized his or her descriptive essay?

A Walk in the Park

Rudy Nevarez

Working the midnight shift as a police officer is not always pleasant. The pressures from the calls for service have accumulated in me, and now it is time that I admitted to myself that I must ask for assistance from my fellow officers. I had an argument with the citizen on the last call, so now I find that my aggressive nature is coming to the surface. At times like these, I have to do something to calm myself down, or I might do something that I would have to apologize for at a later time.

I drive back to the police station and park my car. Since it is now my assigned meal time, I have some free time for myself. I walk into the park where the police station is located, and I take a nocturnal excursion through it. With only the moonlight to illuminate the park, I wander down a winding path. It is so peaceful and serene here, and I feel the presence of a larger spirit, one who obviously cares deeply about his or her natural creations.

The park is full of beauty and peacefulness, yet at times I find evidence of violent human beings. I find the hewn remains of what had once been a lovely tree. Some uncaring soul has chopped this poor tree down so that he or she could use the limbs and trunk for firewood. I can only wish that I'd been there to intervene, to stop the woodcutter from the vandalistic deed.

I climb down to a small gully, using a narrow and winding dirt path. I can see groundwater seeping out of a dirt wall, and the moonlight reflects off this water, making the wall appear to be alive with dancing diamonds. There is a pungent odor of wet, decaying vegetation in the area. I continue along this gully until I reach the switchback; then I make a hard, strenuous climb up to the summit, and, standing riveted at the edge, I admire the inspiring overlook of the park below.

With my peace of mind restored, I would return to my patrol duties to once again face the world.

Beautiful Beach

Leslee Hall

My favorite place to be is Half Moon Bay State Beach. I have fond memories of family trips as a child and much more peaceful memories of myself alone at the beach.

I see the sun reflect off glass particles and send its piercing reflections into my eyes. I think of counting every grain of sand and I laugh out loud. The water changes to every shade of blue imaginable. White foam trims the shore like lace on a tablecloth. It is blown away like little cotton balls and is replenished as quickly as it is diminished. Seaweed is strewn about like rice at a wedding with beautiful, natural shades of green and brown coloring the leaves and the stems. Seagulls slice through the sky like thin graceful blades, showing that they have perfected the art of skydiving like no human ever will. Others float atop the water, disappearing with a wave and reappearing in an instant. Maintaining its plight for survival, a gull appears with a fish.

The iridescent gills reflect a rainbow of colors as the fish hopelessly opens and shuts his mouth. This is the last moment of the fish's existence.

The sound of waves crash around me like thunder in a raging storm. This is one of the most beautiful, but frightening, aspects of nature. In an instant, all is silent. Then, like a stalking animal, an enormous wave leaps across the shore. Moments later, the same calm occurs, and the animal leaps again. A seagull cries to another through the language of Aves, never to be understood. The shrillness of the cry lingers.

The fragrant, yet indescribable, smell of salt is around. It invites itself into your nostrils which is in an odd way refreshing. You can smell the stench of the sea, with its rotting plants and dead animals, creating a smell that makes you wince.

The cool mist enraptures you like a blanket, hitting your face and causing you to draw your breath in quickly. The next mist makes you shut your eyes and inhale deeply, causing you to look forward to the next one. The sand is soft when sifted through your fingers, although the texture of it is coarse when rubbed between your palms. The sun climbs into all corners of your being. Hopeless of escaping it, you instead relish in its beauty and relax on your mattress of custom-formed sand.

All of these surroundings, as a whole, take me away to a place that no man can ever recreate. The reality of the world is always overpowered by the wonder of nature.

The Golden Road

Dave Stieb's love was the freeways, and it wasn't surprising that he grew up in the Los Angeles area—a city where the automobile defines the way of life. He was a young man when I knew him; both of us were freshmen at the University of California at Santa Barbara, and we lived on the same off-campus dormitory floor for that first year. Dave loved to drink, too, and what better place for a drinker than the alcoholic college community of Isla Vista? I really got to know Dave over a nine-month academic year because Dave went back to Cerritos at the end of that year and he never returned to school the next fall.

But did I mention that Dave's love was the freeways? Yes, I think I did. Dave's love was of the multi-lane super-road, the automobile and the freeway's intricate organizational scheme, and if you were to ask Dave what his favorite (or "lucky") numbers were, the chances are good that his response would include the numbers 5, 10, 101, 110, and 605. Dave was a latter-day gypsy, roaming the network of Southern California roads, covering a territory from roughly the Mexican Border in the south to Santa Barbara in the north, and his eyes would gleam and dart each time he would pass one of those numbered signs of the interstate system while cruising. He especially liked the way the colors on those signs—red, white, blue—were just like the colors of the American flag. It really got him excited to talk about it.

Dave was majoring not in geography but in business-economics, and I have since wondered why his major was not geography. He knew directions, that Dave Stieb, and it was impressive to watch him work his stuff out on the road. I remember one instance when we were going to the local 7-11 to buy some beer, and we had to make the choice of one of two routes from our dorm (near Isla Vista) to the store (in Goleta): state highway 217 (a two lane freeway) or the Los Carneros-Hollister city streets. But for Dave Stieb, there was no choice involved; he had already figured out the system, though he'd only been living in Santa Barbara for a few months.

"You see," he would say, as we cruised together in his navy blue 1978 Camaro, "the 217 is at least five minutes faster than Los Carneros-Hollister, and," he would add, smugly, "you'll never find a cop on the 217."

Dave was right. Ever since that day, when I travel to Santa Barbara, I test Dave's theory against the chance that he could be wrong. I must agree with Dave Stieb: the 217 is definitely faster. And I've never seen a cop.

Dave grew up in Cerritos, and he returned there to visit on most weekends. He was something of an enigma on our floor: some people thought he had a girl back home; others thought he hated life away from home; but I know now why Dave Stieb went home on all those weekends; he wanted to drive the roads.

It wasn't so much the pleasure of driving or speed that Dave liked. He was not like one of those speed demons, or drag racers, or drive-by shooters, nor was he a Sunday driver or a "little old lady from Pasadena." Dave enjoyed the system of the roads. Look at it this way:

if Dave Stieb worked for the airlines, he'd be a navigator and not a pilot. He loved to explore the delicate intricacies of the California road system. And he knew all the names and numbers of the freeways in Southern California. He could rattle them off like some elementary school kids recite state capitols: Del Amo, Lakewood Blvd. (19), Bell-flower, Manchester (42); Pacific Coast Highway (1), Santa Monica Blvd. (2), the Golden State Freeway (5), the Christopher Columbus Transcontinental Highway (10). I could just see Dave driving for hours on these roads, stopping occasionally only for food, gas, or beer (Dave was known to enjoy a cold one on the road). When the traffic would slow, I could see him rolling down his window and turning up the Iron Maiden on the car stereo. I could see him opening it up when he got outside the major city zones, pushing the Camaro's needle up to 70 as he motored out through the San Fernando valley towards Santa Barbara.

And even there at school Dave's love for the system was evident. I remember sitting with him at the University Pub, over a pitcher of illegally-purchased beer. It was an overcast day, and we had cut school, deciding instead to ride our bikes to the Pub and hang out. When we had sat down, Dave opened his notebook and, to some degree, his heart.

"You see," he said, "the system of bike paths here at UCSB is a great one, right? So why doesn't somebody step up and give them some names and numbers, you know, like the freeways."

I had to say that I honestly hadn't thought about it. I wondered if anyone had.

"So," he was going on, "here's what I've come up with." He flipped to a page in his notebook and revealed a hand-drawn map of the UCSB campus, with the bike paths drawn in, of course. Assigned to each bike path was a number and a name. "This," he said, beaming, "is what I call IV 1: The Francisco-Torres Parkway, because besides campus, that is it's main destination."

I nodded, amused, and was catching on. I saw a familiar gleam in his eye as he continued.

He went on: "San Rafael-Del Playa" (UCSB Highway 2); the "Library Y" (freeway interchange); and the "Girvetz-Snidecor (business) Loop." He also assigned numbers to each of the major bikeways, all the while sticking to the U.S. interstate's system: odd numbers for north-south routes, even numbers for east-west. He even had the various under- and overpasses named, employing the best name for each: Pardall, Cambell, and Robertson (a street, a lecture hall, and a gymnasium). Dave Stieb had single-handedly—and quite attractively— done what no one else had ever bothered to do: he had organized the bike lanes! As we drank our ill-gotten pitcher, Dave explained his highway patrol, his sign designs (complete with mileage to upcoming destinations), and everything else that made his scheme so amazing. I applauded Dave, silently and to myself.

I don't see Dave much any more. Later that year, Dave challenged another guy from our floor in a harmless three-game set of racquetball. Bets were taken, sides were drawn up, and the whole match turned into a floor-wide spectacle. Dave lost the first two games and then drove home to Cerritos for the weekend. When he returned he told us that he would not be coming back for the next school year, for he was dropping out of college. The racquetball games became known forever as "Dave Stieb's Last Stand"—a standing legend in our circle of friends that are still in touch. I heard that he crashed his Camaro a few years back, and I remember somebody telling me that Dave was working at the Long Beach airport, as a gas jockey.

Last summer he drove down to San Diego to visit a couple of times, and I remember him being pretty loaded when he hopped into his beat-up Mazda to return to Cerritos. Dave was pulled over by the California Highway Patrol on his second trip home. He was charged with a violation of Section 23213.a of the California State Vehicle Code: driving under the influence of alcohol. Dave spent a few hours in jail, blew a .11 B.A.C. into a breathalyzer hose, and lost his license for six months later that year.

He called me just the other day and said he'd been in trouble with the law again, something about driving on a suspended license. Now they'd taken it for two years. Somehow I don't think that matters to Dave; he's gonna drive anyway. Or will he?

———————————

Puerto Penasco

Suzanne Moore

Butterfly shrimp as big as your fist are daily fare in Puerto Penasco, and if you don't mind driving between two and three hundred miles through a 120-degree on a two-lane Mexican highway, it's a wonderful place to vacation.

Nestled on the eastern side of the Sea of Cortez, five and a half hours southeast of Mexicali, lies a wonderful place to escape the daily drudge on the road to happy destiny.

Puerto Penasco is a haven for the retired and tired alike; therefore, seeing travelers snoozing in the shade, each alongside one of the many R.V.'s that line the beaches, is not an unusual sight. What is unusual is that this is a relatively obscure spot, visited mostly by people from Arizona who come down because Puerto Penasco is their closest beach location.

In my case, word of mouth and a very high recommendation initiated my journey. The first impression of Puerto Penasco was rather disappointing, most probably because visually it looks like a lot of Mexican desert towns, arid, dusty, and inhabited by people sorely lacking the material possessions we Americans take for granted.

Even so, the locals are friendly and courteous, always there with a shovel if you happen to get your car stuck in the sand (which I did) on many of the unpaved roads that lead to the locals' favorite beaches.

The tide at the beach rises 18 feet daily. This gives you the choice of either swimming or exploring the tide pools, depending on what time you choose to go. The only trouble is that if you have your tidal charts confused, you may end up carting all of your snorkel gear down to the water only to find there is none.

But don't fret, there are miles of beaches strewn with the largest assortment of seashells I've ever seen. Conch shells are common as are those beautiful brown-and-white striped, spiraling shells that you only see in gift shops.

If you lie down on the warm, white beach and look across the sand horizontally, you can see what appears to be little tubes sticking out of the finely textured sand. These are huge clams the size of which I'm sure you've never imagined. Usually it takes two people because the neck is slimy, and slippery, like Jell-O in water, so while one person holds it, the other person has to dig down under the clam to lift it out.

There is so much to do just on the beach alone. The freedom of walking for miles with nothing to do except smell the salt air, gather nature's bounty and enjoy the sun surrounding you, is unequaled. I could wriggle my toes in the wet sand, plop down and be content to sit there from early in the morning, when the air is still, to the afternoon with its turquoise blue skies and warm winds, to the evening where the stars are so clear they take your breath away.

Every few weeks the winds kick up for one or two days. During this time, the beach isn't an option because the sand gets blown hard against your skin like a thousand tiny needles, and it's difficult to see. So you then do the two next best things: Eat and shop!

If you drive carefully down the dirt road leading out of town, you will see signs for "Cholla Mall." Here there are hundreds of stalls selling every kind of tourist treat you want. But any resemblance to a mall stops there because the stalls are all outside, sardined next to each other with no shelter from the heat except a tarp covering the trinkets, hats, blankets and jewelry. Shopping under these conditions can work up your appetite, and what a great excuse to go back into town to enjoy the local fare in a nice, chilly, air-conditioned restaurant. Because there are so many Americans living and vacationing here, a lot of the food is catered to them.

The water is bottled, and unless you eat at a street corner taco stand, you have a pretty good chance of not getting sick. So, I indulged myself and ate just about everything from seafood to salad to beef flautas. I stayed away from the dairy products, which was a shame because I really wanted to try the "fried ice cream."

All in all, I found Puerto Penasco to be a wonderful place to relax, explore, indulge my appetite, shop without spending a lot and soak up the sunsets in a safe and friendly environment. Anyone looking for a unique vacation would be hard-pressed to find a better place than this little haven on the Sea of Cortez.

CHAPTER FOUR

SENTENCE STRUCTURE

CONSTRUCTING A SENTENCE

Here are two important reasons why you should learn about sentence structure and common sentence errors:

1. As was mentioned in the preceding chapter, it is often necessary to learn a certain vocabulary for the discipline you are studying, and English and writing are no different from other fields of study in this respect. You must learn to call a rose a rose so that you know a rose when you see one; so too should you learn what a sentence fragment is so that you'll know to avoid them. For the student of grammar, this particular concept is simply a matter of your ability to recognize forms. If I held up three circles and one square and asked you to identify the one that did-n't belong, you'd have no trouble at all. Just think of sentence fragments, comma splices, and run-ons in this light; learn their forms and you will be able to spot them in no time (preferably before you turn in a paper!).

2. Because sentence construction is such an elemental part of the English language, it is one of those deficiencies in a person's writing that will stand out the most. Our thoughts form specific patterns in both writing and speech, so you must learn to emulate those patterns to communicate effectively in the English-speaking world. Do not let someone judge you by your basic sentence constructions; learning to avoid the most common errors is easy, but it does take practice.

**Parts
of a Sentence**

These are the terms that you need to know before you can learn about sentence structures. These terms will be used often and interchangeably with one another in this chapter to describe the way sentences are constructed.

1. Subject-Verb

- The subject of the sentence can be compared to an "actor." The subject performs the action of the verb in your sentence.
- The verb of the sentence is the action performed by the subject.

> Some peculiar poets prefer peace of mind to publication.
> SUBJECT   VERB

Notice that the verb (action) in the sentence is "performed" by a person or place. The *poets* are performing an action (*preferring* one thing over another).

2. Independent Clause

- An independent clause is a collection of words that is often expressed as a "complete thought." An independent clause **must** contain a subject and a verb, and each complete sentence must contain at least one independent clause.

> My English teacher taught me everything I know.
> SUBJECT   VERB

3. Dependent Clause

- A dependent clause is a collection of words that may have subjects and verbs, but may not stand alone as a sentence because of a limiting **dependency**.

> When the wind blows

Notice that this is an incomplete thought. The reader still needs to know what happens "when the wind blows."

- Use of dependent clauses without a supporting independent clause is often the cause of a **sentence fragment**.

4. Subordinating Conjunction

- These are one or two word conjunctions that create dependent clauses. The clauses are dependent because in most cases more information is required for the sentence to be complete. To return to the above example.

> <u>When</u> the wind blows

When the wind blows, WHAT? The word "when" indicates that something else is going on simultaneously, so the sentence must be added to:

> <u>When</u> the wind blows, the cradle will rock.
> SUBORDINATING
> CONJUNCTION

Below is a list of the most common subordinating conjunctions:

Subordinating Conjunctions

after	if	though
although	because	while
since	when	until
unless	whether	as if
as	before	why

These conjunctions will be dealt with in greater detail when we discuss sentence patterns and comma usage.

5. Sentence Types

1. Simple (one independent clause)
2. Compound (two or more independent clauses joined by comma and coordinating conjunction)
3. Complex (one subordinate clause and one independent clause)
4. Compound-Complex (one subordinate clause and two or more independent clauses joined by commas and coordinating conjunctions)

Common Sentence Structuring Errors

The three most common structuring errors are **sentence fragment**, **comma splice**, and the **run-on sentence**. Human beings learn to recognize the danger symbols of life, and this is how we survive in a hostile world. We fear the ominous fin of the shark; the rattle and diamond-shaped head of the sidewinder; we know that a hot stove hurts after only one or two experiences burning our hands. Learn to recognize the danger symbols of writing too.

1. Sentence Fragment

- A sentence is a fragment if it is lacking an independent clause. Remember, an independent clause must have both a subject and verb, and be able to stand alone as a complete sentence.
- Most fragments are a result of sentences that lack either subjects or complete verbs, or they may begin with a subordinating conjunction. Here are a few examples of fragmented sentences. Your sentence fragmentation may vary.

> When there was fresh, clean air to breathe.
>
> Could have many moraines or glaciers.
>
> Jane lying dead on the frozen pond.

What must be done to the above sentences to repair their fragmentary state? In real writing situations, it is often most appropriate to attach some fragments to surrounding sentences, but fragments may also be repaired simply by adding the necessary information to them. Check each sentence to make sure that it has both a subject and complete verb.

PRACTICE

Correct the sentence fragments in the paragraph below by adding a subject, verb, or by attaching them to a nearby sentence.

> The surfer died because he chose a wave that was too big for his ability. As he rode down the face. He looked like a tiny speck on a magnificent background of blue. Like a fly on a coffee table. There was a razor sharp coral reef. Waiting like a predatory animal just below the glassy ocean surface. When the surfer hit the water. The crowd gasped. Knowing it was over.

2. Comma Splice

- A comma splice occurs when a writer incorrectly separates two independent clauses with a comma.
- Because independent clauses express complete ideas, they must be separated with one of three punctuation forms: a period, semicolon, or a comma together with a coordinating conjunction.

The seven coordinating conjunctions are: **for**, **and**, **nor**, **but**, **or**, **yet**, **so**.
Here are a few examples of comma splices:

> The land was free, I was a prisoner.
>
> Drugs are for losers, I guess I'm a loser.
>
> Some people call me the Space Cowboy, some call me the Gangster of Love.
>
> —Steve Miller

What must be done to the above sentences to make them correct? To mend the wound created by the comma splice, apply one of the three punctuational rules listed above. Change the comma to a semicolon or period, or add a coordinating conjunction. Now try a few sentences craftily hidden in the paragraph below.

PRACTICE

Correct the comma splices in the paragraph below by changing the punctuation or adding an appropriate conjunction.

> Most people these days are scared to death by computers, this is because they are afraid of pushing the wrong button. Even though this fear is prevalent in our society today, computers are still the primary instrument used in business and industry. I have always been one of those people who is afraid of new technology, I am getting better about using computers and other electronic gadgets like the VCR, voice mail, etc. Education seems to be the answer to society's fears of technology, everyone

should be required to take classes in computers throughout their school careers.

3. The Run-on or Fused Sentence

- A run-on sentence occurs when a writer fails to use appropriate punctuation, or no punctuation at all. These types of errors usually occur when a writer is trying to say too much without using the signposts of writing—punctuation.

Here are some examples of run-on sentences:

> White-collared conservatives are flashing down the street they're pointing their plastic fingers at me.
> —Jimi Hendrix

> This here river don't go to Antree boy you made a wrong turn.
> —Deliverance

> This college has an excellent English program just ask anyone who's been here.

Apply the same method that you used for the comma splice to correct a run-on sentence:

1. Add a period.
2. Add a comma and/or a conjunction.
3. Add a semicolon.

PRACTICE

Correct the run-on sentences in the paragraph below by changing the punctuation or adding an appropriate conjunction.

> What is happening to our young people? It seems that children are not happy with games like hide and seek or kickball all they want to do is to play video games like Nintendo or Sega.

When I was a kid my friends and I would ride our bikes or pretend we were explorers sometimes we would also build forts out of discarded scraps of lumber I think kids need to get away from the T.V. once and awhile and get out and do something that exercises their creativity.

WRITING ASSIGNMENTS

1.   Check your own essay in progress for sentence structure errors such as the comma splice, run-on sentence, or sentence fragment.

Proofread the following paragraphs for errors in sentence structure. Correct fragments, run-ons, and comma splices.

As I arrived at the Halloween party. I immediately noticed a motley-looking gang of hooligans. The walls were covered with these tacky orange and brown computer paper designs someone had obviously spent many hours putting them up. A strobe light was blinking on and off, a DJ was spinning "Monster Mash" while old black and white monster flicks were being played on one blank wall. A bunch of upper classmen in costumes were huddling together. Around the dance floor.

I noticed that many of the students were dancing on the parquet dance floor, I remember this because I found myself trapped among their writhing bodies as I headed for the punch bowl. Some guy in a mummy costume grabbed me he started to twirl me around like a top. I continued to dance with him. Although I was quite dizzy. When he released me. I fell into step with another creepy looking creature he was dressed up like a circuit board. He was a very stiff dancer.

I don't remember how I got home that night, I guess it was just one of those freaky Halloween experiences. I never expected my college life to be so spooky, I suppose that's what they mean by "an intensive program."

CHAPTER FIVE

NARRATIVE WRITING

NARRATION

For some students narration is the easiest writing strategy, yet for others it is the most difficult. Narration in itself is easy to understand. Narration is simply telling a story with a point, a thesis. Your story supports your thesis whatever your thesis happens to be. Writers sometimes use narrative to express feelings about events that have taken place in their lives, or a narrative might be a creative story involving characters and events that are made-up, or fictitious.

While these are only two examples, there are many theses that could be supported using narration. For example, student writer Rudy Nevarez uses narration in his essay "He Laughed First" to illustrate a humorous event, to make his reader laugh. His narrative appears at the end of this chapter. Writers may also describe pain, suffering, triumph, or courage in narrative essays, and a good narrative expresses some kind of person undergoing a significant action during a certain period of time.

Fiction or Nonfiction?

As a writer you must decide which of two types of narration will be support your thesis. When a writer makes up the characters and events of the story, the narration is called **fiction**. When the characters and events are real, as in the essay "Over the Rainbow," the narration is called a **nonfiction**. Since fictions are not related from personal experience, the writer has more flexibility to invent specific people and events that support his or her thesis. This type of freedom, however, can also be a burden. Many students find that writing nonfiction is easier since they can draw from their personal experiences to support their thesis. Either of these styles is an example of narrative writing.

Directly Stated Thesis vs. Implied Thesis

When writing a narration an author has to choose how her or his thesis will be presented. In expository writing, the kind you will do for most of your classes, a directly stated thesis is always preferred while in fiction writing the implied thesis allows the author stylistic freedom. Often times writers will combine the two forms.

Your instructor can help you choose between the two when you are writing a narration. Both approaches have advantages and disadvantages.

Directly Stated Thesis

In most of your writing you will want to use a directly stated thesis. This type of thesis is one in which you explain to the reader your position on the topic at hand.

> A comparison between the earth's air quality of today and the earth's air quality of fifty years ago will show a significant increase in the amount of toxins present in our atmosphere. Besides making our air more difficult to breathe and causing respiratory problems for those who never had them, acid rain is killing off vegetation. <u>For these reasons, stricter air quality control standards and laws need to be formulated, passed, and enforced.</u>

It is clear the above writer intends to argue for the writing, passing, and enforcing of stricter air quality standards because of the reasons listed in the paragraph. The underlined sentence is a directly stated thesis.

In narrative writing, many writers consider the directly stated thesis a cumbersome interruption in their writing. Therefore, writers often choose to imply their thesis.

Implied Thesis

Though a directly stated thesis clearly explains the author's purpose for writing the essay, writers of narration will often choose for stylistic reasons to imply the thesis. An implied thesis is one in which the author's use of details impies, or suggests, his or her purpose.

> As he adjusted the flow of oxygen on his respirator, he remembered a time you could look over the valley and see for miles.

> Now a thick, black fog clouded the vista. He coughed hard, his whole body shaking in pain. The noon sun appeared a dim, dull orange through the murkiness. His bloodshot eyes followed a dirty, gray bird around the ridge of the canyon he rested on. Soon the rain would come, and what green the summer haze hadn't killed, the hot rain would burn away. He shook his head slowly and sighed.

Through the writer's details, it seems clear that the polluted air and landscape is not desirable. The writer's thesis, however, is not directly stated. We can only infer the writer's attitude toward the issue from the types of details the writer chooses to give us.

The disadvantage of an implied thesis is that the reader may not readily know the author's position on the topic, so when employing an implied thesis, the whole work usually represents the author's complete intentions.

While an implied thesis is especially effective in fiction writing because it allows the writer to maintain an uninterrupted flow of narration, students will often use a directly stated thesis after a narrated opening. This combination allows the student to use narration for effect while avoiding confusion by stating directly his or her thesis.

> My grandfather and I hiked to the top of a ridge he hasn't returned to since he was a boy. As he adjusted the flow of oxygen on his respirator, he remembered a time you could look over the valley and see for miles. Now a thick, black fog clouded the vista. He coughed hard, his whole body shaking in pain. The noon sun appeared a dim, dull orange through the murkiness. His bloodshot eyes followed a dirty, gray bird around the ridge of the canyon we rested on. Soon the rain would come, and what green the summer haze hadn't killed, the hot rain would burn away. My grandfather shook his head slowly and sighed. I couldn't help but conclude that stricter laws regarding air quality control need to be implemented.

The author has combined narration and a directly stated thesis to appeal to the reader's moral sense and to state clearly his or her position on the topic.

Use Chronological Order

In narrative writing the order in which the events happen is referred to as chronology. Chronology is what makes the story clear. For example, if you were writing about how you learned to drive a car, you wouldn't want to start the story with your driving test. Instead, you would probably start with your first time behind the wheel and how whoever was teaching you clutched the dashboard, knuckles turning white, sweat dripping from her brow.

At the same time, you don't want to begin your narrative so far back in the past that the events have no bearing on the point you wish to make. Your responsibility as a writer is to decide where your story begins. It is best to begin the story when the action begins. Continuing the driving example from above, the writer does not need to waste time explaining why he wanted to learn to drive or describing the details of his morning. He starts with the experience and goes from there, describing the experience in detail.

> My first driving experience was a harrowing one. While cruising a country road, my father asked me if I wanted to drive, and I enthusiastically accepted the challenge. I could tell he was nervous, but he surrendered the controls to me. I gingerly slid into the driver's seat and promptly stalled the car. Dad said, "Let it out slowly next time," and after two or three more attempts (with gears grinding loudly), I finally got the car rolling. I drove around for half an hour, nearly driving us both headlong into a deep ditch, before my father took over once again.

One technique writers of fiction employ is the **flash-forward** to begin the story. A flash-forward simply means to begin your narrative with the ending. The desired effect of this technique is to get the reader to focus on the events of the story rather than the ending. In tragedies the hero often dies at the end of the story, but this knowledge is given to the reader up front. If the reader knows the ending in advance, then the details of the story take on a deeper significance so that the reader sympathizes with the hero. As the reader reads on, he or she knows this is the hero's last kiss, last sea voyage, last fight. Only use this technique if you can justify its use beyond novelty. Your reader might, otherwise, find you divisive and distrust your writing.

> "Oh my god! Look out for that ditch!" my father screamed as the tires squealed, my foot stamping down on the brake pedal. The car skidded to a stop bare inches from what appeared to be a ten-foot deep ditch by the side of old Bone Hollow Road. "Get out," he said shakily, "I'm taking over."
>
> But the near-tragic end of this experience only served to bring Dad and me closer together. It all began when we pulled out of that service station on Highway 61. While cruising a country road, my father asked me if I wanted to drive, and I enthusiastically accepted the challenge. I could tell he was nervous, but he surrendered the controls to me. I gingerly slid into the driver's seat and promptly stalled the car. Dad said, "Let it out slowly next time," and after two or three more attempts (with gears grinding loudly), I finally got the car rolling. . . .

May times, however, writers will start their narration with the ending, or experiment with the sequence of events for a desired effect. This technique, sometimes called the **flashback**, is a well-worn trick used in movies, television, and literature. This is an acceptable approach but keep in mind that the more you change the order of the events, the more chances you create for confusion.

Choose a Point of View

As the writer of a narrative, you'll have to decide from which point of view you wish to tell the story. Most student essays are written in first person. That is when the main character in the narration refers to himself or herself as "I." Sometimes, however, students will choose to write in third person, using *he* or *she* instead of *I*. Don Hom's essay "Over the Rainbow" is written in third person even though it is an account of his life in the army. Choose a point of view that comes naturally to you and stick to that point of view throughout your narration. Please refer to Chapter 12 for a detailed analysis of **point of view**.

Develop Your Characters

Another thing you'll want to be sure to include in your narration is character development. Use descriptive details as a way to develop your characters. Choose the details carefully. What is it that makes each character unique? Is it their clothes, an interesting scar, the way they smell, walk, laugh?

Often the way people talk tells more about them than anything else, so dialogue is an easy and effective way to reveal the nature of your characters. Most narratives are a combination of description and **storytelling**, and it is this combination of writing style which can make it challenging to write and enjoyable to read.

Characters in your essays should go beyond cardboard cutouts. Try to use selective, descriptive details and dialogue to make your characters as true to life as possible. Compare the following two examples.

> A. Henry dressed sloppily and spoke with a California accent.
>
> B. Henry's plaid shirt was tucked half in, and his hole-ridden jeans needed washing. His oily hair pointed in all directions. He adjusted his footing on his skateboard as he said, "Hey man, that's cool."

Instead of just telling the reader about Henry, the writer of example <u>B</u> shows the reader what Henry is like through descriptive details and dialogue. If the writer were to continue this description, Henry's mannerism would become apparent, and Henry would appear to the reader as a more realistic character.

Find the details that best describe the person in your narrative and intersperse your essay with these details. This may take some hard work and revision, but in the end your effort will reward you.

Answer the following questions with 2–3 complete sentences.

1. According to the chapter, what is **narration?** How does this style of writing differ from description?

2. What is the difference between **fiction** and **nonfiction?** Which do most students find easier to write and why?

3. Briefly explain the difference between the **implied thesis** and the **directly stated thesis**. Which works best and why?

4. What is **chronological order?** Why is it important to write narratives in this form?

5. According to the chapter, what is **point of view?** Why is the point of view an important consideration in the writing of a narrative essay?

6. List some ideas that you have for a narrative essay of your own. Go on, this one's a free-bee!

VOCABULARY—NARRATION

	Words:

1. exhilarating

2. picturesque

3. effect

4. extraordinary

5. chronological

6. embarrassment

7. castigate

8. significant

9. affect

10. flashback

1. Look up the preceding words in your dictionary. Write down the most meaningful definition <u>and</u> the PART OF SPEECH. Now write the words in sentences to show their meanings.

2. Using your dictionary, work with a small group to write a 2–3 paragraph description or story. Try to use all of the vocabulary words from the list on page 67 in your sentences. Make sure that each sentence follows logically from the previous person's.

3. Define the words from above by their context from the readings. Are there any other uses or meanings for these words?

WRITING ASSIGNMENTS

1. Describe an event from your life in which you displayed extraordinary courage or heroism. How or why was this action important to your life?

2. Recall a particularly embarrassing event in your life. Describe the events that led up to your embarrassment and any consequences that may've followed.

Read the following writing samples, then answer the questions that follow with 2–3 complete sentences.

1. Identify a directly stated thesis from one of the preceding essays. Do any of the essays contain an implied thesis?

2. Outline the order of events in the preceding stories. Do they use chronological order or flashbacks?

3. Identify and describe any characters from the preceding narratives. How do they add to the stories?

He Laughed First

Rudy Nevarez

The park is normally peaceful and calm at night, but it can throw you off a bit, for it is surreal and certainly nothing like the real world of a police office. One night, after a quiet moonlight stroll through the park's meadows, I got a call of a silent alarm at the Art's Council Building that is located near our station house. Upon my arrival, I admired the picturesque building standing amid a backdrop of red-wood trees. Compared to the police station, with its modern day structure and wide array of communications antennas, this building has a rustic look, a certain charm.

Much to my dismay, Officer Smith was the other officer assigned to this call. Officer Smith believes that he is God's gift to the rookie officer—forever pointing out your mistakes so that everyone knows when you have erred. To hear him tell it, he is the strongest and toughest officer in the department. He even likes to tell people that "Dirty Harry" is a pussycat compared to him.

As I approached the building, I saw that Officer Smith had already arrived on the scene and was gesticulating towards the front door of the place. My state of consciousness rose as soon as I realized that the front door was open. Because it was open, we would have to systematically search the building, for we had no idea where the suspect might be at that moment. Knowing that the building had once housed the criminally insane (it was a subdivision of the police station back in the early part of the century) did not help ease the tension of the situation either, and I could recall more than a few ghost stories that were told to me by other officers who had made calls to the place.

With our senses at an extraordinary level of awareness, we entered the building with guns drawn, prepared for the worst. With Smith covering the hallways, I did a quick search of the individual rooms. I slowly eased myself through an open doorway. Suddenly, alarms went off deep in my head, screaming "DANGER!" Through the corner of my eye, I spotted a darkened figure in the shadows with a gun in his hands, and with my heart pounding in my chest and with a baseball-lump in my throat, I spun towards the figure and prepared for mortal combat. As the light from my flashlight hit the figure, I was startled to realize that I had almost shot my reflection in a mirror that was a part of an exhibit. When I finally got my control back, I went back out to the hallway where I found Officer Smith quietly snickering at me. I must have unknowingly sounded out in fright. I went to the next room where I found several objects strewn around the floor. Thinking that possibly someone else may be in the building, we radioed for additional personnel to set up a perimeter around the building.

After the perimeter had been set up, we resumed our search. The first floor was clear, so we started up the winding stairs towards the second floor. As I made the turn onto the first landing, I immediately spotted two figures sitting on a couple of chairs. I yelled at them to raise their hands up, but when they failed to respond, I realized that these two figures, which had succeeded in scaring the daylights out of me, were just a couple of dummies used for an exhibit. Some perverted artist had set them there on display. Once again, from behind me, Officer Smith quietly laughed. He said he knew about the dummies, so he let me go first, just to get a jump. Ha-Ha.

We concluded the search of the second floor but found nothing. As I opened the front door to leave, a huge black cat, who had been hiding behind some old boxes, burst through the door between Smith and me. The suddenness of its appearance and the creepy screech that it let out stopped me in my tracks for a moment, leaving me with a cold, corpse-like feeling. Once I'd recovered, I moved to leave, but I found my path blocked by an unmoving Officer Smith. I looked into his face just in time to see a look of utter terror replaced by an expression of pure embarrassment. In the dim light of the moon I could see a wet patch slowly growing around Smith's crotch, and a small puddle was forming from a trickle out of his pant leg. Howling with laughter, and glad to be out of that spooky house, I advised dispatch that I was back in service, but that Officer Smith would be en-route to the station for a change of pants.

Over the Rainbow

Don Hom

The sweat trickled down his camouflaged face as he crept down the jungle trail. The sweet stench of the rotting underbrush filled his nostrils. He scanned the surrounding area. Nothing. Man, he thought, there ain't nothing out here. Not a trace of these Chinchineros, or

Rancheros or Doritos or whatever they call these friggin' guerrillas. That's it, Don, get complacent. Just like the helicopter crew did only about a week earlier. They had landed in a clearing to stretch out a little and the next thing they knew they were face down in a ditch. Dead. Executed. Placed on their knees and shot in the back of the neck, their faces barely recognizable by their own families. Yeah, he thought, keep thinking that way and you'll end up just like them, Donnie boy. Pay attention, he screamed silently to himself. Scan. Getting hot. Hard to breathe too. He'd been through jungle warfare school in Panama, and even though it was difficult terrain, it was nothing like Honduran jungle. All mountains here. High rain forest, he guessed, you'd call it, and the air was thin.

CRACK! Freeze! Holy shit, you gotta be kidding me! Didn't sound like an AK-47; didn't sound like an M-16 either, which is what most of them carried. How ironic that the men they were hunting carried tools of death made by his own country. Sounded like a small caliber rifle. A .22 maybe? He looked back at the squad leader, Sergeant Lucas, for instructions. The Sergeant signaled him to proceed cautiously with a small hand movement. Spoken words are not necessary when they could be your last. The shot came from about their one o'clock, or at least he thought it did. No way to tell in these freaking jungle draws. There's a clearing over that way. Oh, jeez, man, why did I ever enlist to do this kind of crap? Being a tough guy means nothing when you're dead.

The sweat really began to flow. His heart beat like a bass drum.

Quicker. Harder. Until he thought that it would jump right out of his chest. 'Bout a hundred meters now. O hot damn, there's someone out there. Latino male. Damn, this is not supposed to happen, man. We're just here to train, right? Just a deterrent like the nuclear bombs, right? Weapon up. Gotta go slow now, Donnie. Make sure you get the jump. Initiative they call it. Identify . . . friendly or enemy. Don't want to go blowing away some civilian. Then you'd really be in world of shit. Whew! Just a farmer with a rifle, hunting maybe, but you never know. His body stiffened and he raised his clenched right hand above his head to signal the squad to freeze. Then he opened his hand to signal them to take a knee. Sergeant Lucas came forward to assess the situation. Smart man, Sergeant Lucas. If anyone can get us out of this in one piece, he's the man. He spent two tours in Vietnam. Yeah, smart man, or maybe not so smart. The sergeant signaled to send up Fernandez, point man. He was sending him out to talk to the farmer. What? Me too? Shit, man, it's always me—the price you pay for doing your job right.

He and Fernandez walked out of the jungle and into the blinding reality of the sunlight. Fernandez yelled something in Spanish. The farmer looked in their direction, but he made no move with the .22. The rest of the soldiers were waved forward.

The farmer and Fernandez spoke. Come on, Ferny, make it quick. I feel like a pop-up out here. He watched as Fernandez continued to talk, trying to keep his eyes on a thousand places at once. Finally, they shook, smiled and exchanged their parting words. What'd he say,

Fern? Says he knew about the Cinchineros, but he's just trying to scare a jaguar that was going after his cow.

Sergeant Lucas welcomed them back into the perimeter that the squad had secured with his usual stern, weathered look. He and Fernandez spoke:

"Hom," he said, "you and Smith are gonna pull LPOP [Listening and Observation Post] tonight about 1 click from the patrol base. You two will split from us and look for a good location. Check?"

"Check," he sighed.

They watched as the squad ambled away through the jungle. As the surrounding jungle began to darken, they looked at each other like two children lost in a department store.

Night surrounded them. "Hey, Smith," he whispered.

"Yeah."

"You take first watch and wake me at oh-one-thirty, okay?" As team leader, he was responsible for the late watch. With a deafening quiet in the jungle around him, he settled into the warmth of the soil. Smith took the watch.

"Psst. Hom. Psst." Someone whispering breath, warm in his ears. The sweat from his sleep caused a chill to course through his body. It was Smith, of course. You're up, man."

He tried to wipe the sleep from his eyes only to realize that he could not see his own hand as he touched his face. Gonna have to pull out the ole NOD's [Night Optical Device]. Ahh, much better, infra-red vision at its best. Just like daytime. Those bastards can never slip on you, slit your throat, with these babies on. Why am I here? No one back home would believe this shit. Home. McDonalds. Baseball. Football. Girls. Not much of that here. . . .

He used his ears to peer out into the jungle, straining them. Nothing. Boring. Never knew what Dorothy from *The Wizard of Oz* meant, or felt like, until now. No place like home, there's no place like home. He chuckled silently to himself. Oh yeah, now I know, now I know. Lisa, so far away. Long, flowing red hair, curly, smells like a piece of heaven. What was she doing without him right now. It hurt to think.

He sat alone in the blackened jungle, Smith snoozing beside him, waiting for the dawn. Sometime later, it arrived.

The Fist of Hell

For a third grader the world is a limited place. I was attending Our Lady of Grace, a private, Catholic school. My view of the world didn't extend beyond the justice and discipline we were taught, but when I moved to Livermore in the middle of third grade, my comfortable, naive view of the world came to an end.

At Our Lady of Grace the rules were strict, and infractions were dealt with harshly. The worse punishment a third grader had to face was a visit to the Mother Superior. She was an old, venerable women, who wore black robes and a scowl on her face. With just a look she could bring the meanest kid to his knees, praying to God to let him please live to see another day. Everyone in the third grade believed that Mother Superior had a direct link to God. It was rumored that she could ask God to damn you for the rest of your life, and He would. When she walked the halls, everyone was silent, even the other nuns.

What kind of horrible crime would it take for one to be sent to Mother Superior? Simply, talking back to any of the nuns, or disrupting the class, or not playing fairly during recess were reasons enough to warrant a visit to Mother Superior. Her way of discipline involved humiliation in front of your peers and parents. I remember one time a student was talking to me. I asked him to be quiet and got caught telling him so. My punishment was the removal of my picture from the Honor Roll board in the hall. My parents were coming to open house that night and expected to see my picture on the wall because I had bragged about it. I had some red-faced explaining to do.

In third grade I was not old enough to distinguish the difference between respect and fear. Looking back now, I realize that what we felt for Mother Superior was not respect but fear. Fear and humiliation were what helped keep the trouble makers in line, yet there was never any physical violence. I suppose humiliation in front of parents and friends and the threat of God damning us to hell before we even had a chance to be rebellious was enough.

My whole world consisted of following strict rules with harsh punishments. One thing I had always wanted at Our Lady of Grace was to sit in the front row. Tall for a third grader, I always had to sit in the back. My vision wasn't the greatest, so it was hard for me to see the board. Besides, the students who got to sit in the front row seemed special. I never, however, went against the wishes of the nun teaching the class. I always sat where I was told.

When my family moved to Livermore, I was sad to leave my school because I was familiar with the way things were done, and I was not a bad student. Since I understood the rules and punishments, I left feeling that the nuns had treated me fairly. Everyone was treated the same, good students and troublesome ones alike. Because of my limited experiences, I also thought that the rules and punishments would be the same at my new school. I was sorely mistaken.

I arrived in my new class a bit late because we had to find the school. I thought the teacher, Mrs. Wood, might castigate me, but instead she greeted me with a smile and introduced me to the class. There was an open desk in the first row and I was anxious to see if I would sit there. Mrs. Wood considered it for a moment, but then moved the boy in the second desk up a row. She said I was too tall for the front and she wanted to keep her eye on Jimmy. I was pleased. This was the closest I had ever gotten to the front row.

As I settled down with my pencils and notebooks, I noticed that most of the class was paying attention to the teacher, but many students weren't. In fact, when Jimmy turned around to talk to me, I began to realize things in this school were different.

"Gee, you're awfully tall," he turned to me and said.

Jimmy had scabs and scars on his face. His teeth were crusty, and his head was shaven and nicked at odd angles. He had a split lip and wild eyes. He was the ugliest person I had ever seen.

"Yes," I said nervously. I didn't want to talk in class while the teacher was writing on the board. "I've always been too tall to sit in the front row."

"Well, let's change places, so you can see what it's like in the front," Jimmy said enthusiastically.

"Are you sure we won't get in trouble?" I asked.

"No problem," he reassured me.

How nice this Jimmy was! He was willing to give up his place in the front row to me. I really liked this new school even though their methods were very strange to me.

As the teacher lectured with her back to us, Billy and I switched places. I was in paradise. I felt a sense of confidence I had never felt before. I was proud and sat straight up. When Mrs. Wood turned around, it didn't take her a moment to notice the switch since I was sitting up so tall.

"I told you I wanted you sitting behind Jimmy," she scolded me. This was more like what I was used to. Dejectedly I picked up my things, ready to switch back with Jimmy. As I stood up he told me to stay. He wasn't going to move. I hesitated.

"Jimmy," Mrs. Wood demanded, "I want you in the front row.

This time I did not hesitate. I stood next to the desk and waited for Jimmy to move. He glared at me. He glared at Mrs. Wood. He glared at all of us. What strange world had I entered?

After we switched places, again, I decided it would be best if I just paid attention to Mrs. Wood's lecturing. She turned to the side board farthest from Jimmy and me.

Jimmy turned to me to talk. I kept me eyes fixed on Mrs. Wood while he spoke and nodded in agreement to the things he said. I had perfected this technique at Our Lady of Grace. Apparently, Jimmy wanted my full attention. The next thing I felt was my neck snapping back. As I reeled forward, my lip went numb. I swam in a daze as I looked at Billy.

"Why did you do that?" I asked.

He simply shrugged his shoulders and turned around.

Then a drop of blood fell onto my desk. No one had said a word to Mrs. Wood who still was writing on the board. Well, I guessed I would have to tell her myself. I got up and walked slowly across the room toward her, my lip getting bigger and bigger. The class watched closely. They made me uncomfortable, but Jimmy would pay for his actions.

As I approached Mrs. Wood she loomed larger and larger. Why hadn't the class screamed out at this injustice? At Our Lady of Grace something like this had only happened once or twice before, and the students watching screamed in terror. The student who had done the hitting was reportedly never seen again, and there was mention of eternal damnation.

My steps got slower as the class watched me. They pointed at me and began to laugh. It was as if I had done something wrong. When I reached Mrs. Wood, I couldn't have taken another step. Before I could tug on her dress, she turned to see what everyone was laughing at. There she towered above me. "Yes, what is it?" she asked sternly.

I mustered up all my courage. "Jimmy hit me," I said.

"Well," she replied, "he's like that sometimes." Then she turned back to the board and continued writing.

Half the class pointed and made comments. The other half ignored me as I walked back in fear to my desk, but this fear was different than the kind at Our Lady of Grace. This fear did not contain a justice for all. As I climbed into my desk with Jimmy smiling as I passed him, I suddenly realized I was in a world that made no sense, a world strange and incomprehensible. A world I would have to learn to live in. I truly was in hell.

CHAPTER SIX

COMMAS AND CONJUNCTIONS

INTRODUCTION

Why it is important to know commas thoroughly:

1. Commas, and all punctuation, are the street signs of writing. Commas, periods, and semi-colons tell us how to proceed, where to go, how fast, and when to stop. You must use punctuation correctly to be an effective writer.
2. The comma is often used in the construction of sentences. When used correctly, errors such as the comma splice, sentence fragment, and run-on sentence may be eliminated!
3. Most importantly, however, a skilled writer uses the comma to provide variety of style. Commas allow a writer to use differing sentence patterns which enhance the appearance of written prose.

COORDINATION

Coordination is the bringing together of two independent clauses by using a comma and a coordinating conjunction. Recall the 7 coordinating conjunctions:

Coordinating Conjunctions

For	But
And	Or
Nor	Yet
	So

These conjunctions are easily remembered by the acronym F.A.N.B.O.Y.S. These letters represent the letters of each conjunction. Before you begin using coordinating conjunctions, however, it is important to know the meanings of each of them:

FOR means because, or as a result of

> I warned him of the danger, <u>for</u> I knew what lay ahead.

AND means also, or in addition to. To use *and*, and both conditions expressed by the independent clauses must be true.

> I fought the law, <u>and</u>the law won.
>
> —The Bobby Fuller Four

NOR is sometimes used with the adjective *neither* and expresses negativity.

> I didn't know the way, <u>nor</u> did I really care.

BUT means to express an opposing idea. When *but* is used, the first clause generally differs significantly from the second.

> I shot the sheriff, <u>but</u> I did not shoot the deputy.
>
> —Bob Marley

OR means that either clause may be true. As opposed to *and* where both cases must be true, *or* validates either one.

> Give me the gun, <u>or</u> I will call the police.

YET means the same thing as but. That is to say, *yet* also indicates conflicting or contrary ideas working in the two clauses.

> I love the game of baseball, <u>yet</u> I cannot play it well

SO means as a result of. Usually this conjunction is used in cause-effect relationships. The idea expressed in the first clause will lead to that expressed in the second.

I love animals, <u>so</u> I went to the zoo.

To use coordination, simply place the appropriate conjunction, preceded by a comma, between the two independent clauses. Now you have a **compound sentence**.

I shot the sheriff. I did not shoot the deputy.

becomes . . .

I shot the sheriff, but I did not shoot the deputy.
—Bob Marley

PRACTICE

1. Determine the relationship between the following sentences, and then join them using a comma and coordinating conjunction.

A. The door was locked tight. I broke the window to get in.

    _____

    _____

    _____

    _____

B. Jack had many enemies in the world. He buried the treasure in a secret location.

    _____

    _____

    _____

    _____

C. The man-eating fern was no longer hungry. It had just eaten the tasty secret agent from Mexico.

    _____

    _____

    _____

    _____

2. Complete the following sentences by adding a comma, coordinating conjunction, and a second independent clause. Try to use each coordinating conjunction at least once.

A. I can't stand my Algebra class

B. He locked the cat and dog in the bathroom together

C. My sister loves to go to Giants games

D. Althea follows her favorite band everywhere

E. Professional baseball players should not be paid so much money

F. I could not stand to watch the little girl vomit in that old movie, *The Exorcist*

G. The 1996 Olympics were held in Atlanta, Georgia

3. **WRITING ACTIVITY:** Now that you have had sufficient practice with coordination, write 5 compound sentences for your essay in-progress. You may choose existing simple sentences, or you may create new ones. These sentences should relate to the subject you're writing about because they will be inserted right into the work when you revise for the final product. Try to use a variety of coordinating conjunctions, and don't forget those commas!

SUBORDINATION

Subordination is the bringing together of one independent clause with a dependent clause to make a complex sentence. A dependent clause begins with a subordinating conjunction. Recall the most common subordinating conjunctions:

Common Subordinating Conjunctions

after	because	unless
although	before	until
as	if	when
as if	since	whether
even though	though	why

Like coordinating conjunctions, these subordinating conjunctions have important meanings that will help you to understand the situations in which they are used. Let's take a look at a few of them:

AFTER indicates that the dependent clause is introducing an event that happened before the one expressed in the subsequent independent clause.

> After I went fishing, I had to wash scales from my hair.

ALTHOUGH indicates contrasting ideas. This conjunction can be compared to the coordinating conjunction *but*.

> Although the girl was quite ugly, Tom asked her out anyway.

AS indicates two events that happen or have happened at the same time.

> I was awestruck by the enormous skyscrapers as I walked through downtown San Francisco.

BECAUSE indicates cause and effect. The action in the dependent clause directly causes or leads to the action in the independent clause.

> Because the stereo was blaring, Ken did not hear the gunshots.

SINCE indicates an ongoing continuous action. This conjunction may also be synonymous with *because* (see above).

> Since I was ten, I have always wanted to be a pilot.

or . . .

> Since he was riding in the back of the truck, he was soaked by the sudden downpour of rain.

WHEN indicates two actions occurring simultaneously. This conjunction is very similar to *as*.

> When Eller pointed the gun at the lion's head, it roared.

To use subordination, begin the sentence with a subordinating conjunction (listed above). This will create a dependent clause. At the end of the dependent clause, place a comma and begin the independent clause. You will know you've reached the end of the dependent clause when the subject of the independent clause appears. Thus:

> I read the adventure story. My imagination ran wild.

becomes . . .

> <u>As</u> I read the adventure story, my imagination ran wild.

Notice how a comma is placed in the spot where the period was used before. Like coordination, subordination allows a writer to combine shorter, simple sentences into longer, more meaningful ones. Remember that sentences need an independent clause to be considered complete. Now try these:

PRACTICE

1. Determine the relationship between the following sentence pairs, and then join them by using subordination. Use the conjunctions listed above. Don't forget the comma!

A. Alice fell down the rabbit hole and saw Wonderland. She was never the same little girl.

_____

_____

_____

B. The Cheshire Cat grinned down at her from a twisted tree. Alice strained her eyes to try to see him.

_____

_____

_____

C. Alice entered the mushroom garden. She immediately noticed a caterpillar sitting on one of them.

_____

_____

_____

2. Complete the following sentences by adding a comma and an independent clause. Your sentences must make sense within the context of the subordinating conjunction.

A.   Because Darth Vader was so tall.

B.   Although the Rebel Alliance was small in numbers

C.   When the two fighters engaged in battle.

D.   If the space station had not been destroyed

E.   Since the robot could speak three hundred languages

F.   As Han Solo entered the strange bar in the foreign port of Mos Eisley

3.   **WRITING ACTIVITY:** Now that you have had sufficient practice with subordination, write 5 compound sentences for your essay in-progress. You may choose existing simple sentences, or you may create new ones. These sentences should relate to the subject you're writing about because they will be inserted right into the work when you revise for the final product. Try to use a variety of coordinating conjunctions, and don't forget those commas!

COORDINATION/SUBORDINATION EXERCISE

Use the appropriate coordinating or subordinating conjunction to join these sentences. Remember to use the appropriate punctuation.

1.   He didn't answer the phone. He was in the shower.
2.   He got out of the shower. He dried off.
3.   She will call back. She will come over.
4.   She was in the yard. She didn't hear the knock at the door.
5.   The flowers bloomed brightly. The grass was brown.
6.   First she did her homework. Then she went out for ice cream.
7.   I like Virginia Woolf's novels. She portrays the human condition.
8.   The party was very lively. I was bored.
9.   She caught the ball. They won the game.
10. I cooked her dinner. She was very happy.
11. Tito wasn't at work. Was he at school.
12. They can speak two languages. Finding a job will be easier.
13. I like cake. I don't like frosting.
14. Melissa was very sad. She took a walk to cheer up.
15. You will pass. You will fail.
16. He didn't want to go to dinner. He didn't want to go to the movie.
17. I was late for work. The bus never showed up.
18. He said he loved her. He treated her terribly.
19. She is beautiful. She is smart.
20. He will finish his degree. He will die trying to do it.
21. Harold walked with a limp. He injured himself skiing.
22. The boy wants the bike. His parents don't have the money.
23. He lost his car in the fire. She lost her house.
24. The deficit was reduced. The president was re-elected.
25. He got a flat tire. He couldn't finish the race.

26. She listens to the soothing music. She falls asleep.
27. We go fishing on Saturdays. We didn't go today because of the weather.
28. He likes the car. He doesn't want to buy it.
29. He bats with his right hand. He throws with his left.
30. Sharon enjoys bicycle riding. She has never been on a horse.

REVIEW/PROOFREADING—COORDINATION AND SUBORDINATION

Place or delete commas in the following paragraphs as needed. Look for coordinating and subordinating conjunctions.

Dear Bob,

As you know, baseball season is just around the corner and I have already purchased my season tickets. I keep seeing all of these hokey "rah-rah" type commercials for the Giants but I am still excited about this team. When I was a kid I would always go to their games with my dad and he would buy me Cracker Jacks and himself a beer or two. Sally and I took the kids to a game last year, and paid nearly thirty bucks for dinner. My how times have changed, hey Bob?

Regardless of ticket prices, the season promises good times ahead. With their new player acquisitions the management has promised a pennant in the new National League West division for the rest of the teams are not that strong. People around here are predicting that either the Giants will finish first by virtue of their hitting or they will finish last because of inconsistent pitching. As opening day draws near, I get more, and more excited.

Hope your Padres have a good season too. We're all rooting for them to get out of the cellar someday. Sally and I were sorry to hear about your recent run-in with the law but we can understand why you felt you had to try to burn down the stadium there in San Diego. Hey, arson isn't really that serious. it's not like you killed anyone. . . .

Best of luck to you and yours this new season!

QUIZ—COORDINATION AND SUBORDINATION

1. Write five sentences **in a paragraph** using the coordinating conjunctions AND, BUT, OR, YET, and SO.

2. Write five sentences **in a paragraph** using the subordinating conjunctions ALTHOUGH, BECAUSE, SINCE, WHEN, and AS.

CHAPTER SEVEN

COMPARATIVE ANALYSIS

COMPARING AND CONTRASTING

An effective writing strategy often used by writers is comparison/contrast. When we think comparatively, it helps us see problems more clearly and helps us choose more effectively. For instance, you may be deciding to transfer to another city but are unsure that the change would be beneficial. To help you make the decision to move or to stay, you would compare and contrast certain points about both cities. By using comparison/contrast you could choose with more confidence the city best suited to your relocating needs.

In writing, comparison/contrast is an organizational strategy used to support a thesis. Whether you compare points or contrast them, the comparison that is taking place is in support of the idea you are trying to get across. You can use comparison/contrast to point out humorous characteristics about people as Michael Lema does in "Computer Literate or Illiterate" or to show how two civil rights leaders fought for equality in different ways as Jessica Hammond does in her essay "A Dream versus a Nightmare."

To make a comparison/contrast essay as interesting as possible, we usually compare the similarities of seemingly unsimilar subjects and contrast the points of seemingly similar subjects. For example, you might want to compare the similarities between pro life and pro choice activists to show that each group has more in common than they care to admit. You could contrast television movies to movies on the big screen to show how both mediums are vastly different even though they seem nearly the same. But before you begin your essay, you must decide what your main topics will be and decide how you will compare each topic. These are known as the **points of comparison**.

Organization

There are three methods of organizing the points of comparison with the major topics. These methods are known as **point by point, block by block**, and **mixed**.

1. Point by Point

This organizational method allows the writer to alternate his or her points of comparison on each topic. You can use these points as the foundation of your essay. Let's say you wanted to compare the countercultures of the 1970s and the 1990s. You would have to brainstorm several things by which to compare the two decades. Here are some possible examples for the bases of comparison.

Point by Point Organizational Method

Main Topic 1: 1970s
First point of comparison: *Fashions*
Main Topic 2: 1990s
First point of comparison: *Fashions*

Main Topic 1: 1970s
Second point of comparison: *Drugs*
Main Topic 2: 1990s
Second point of comparison: *Drugs*

Main Topic 1: 1970s
Third point of comparison: *Music*
Main Topic 2: 1990s
Third point of comparison: *Music*

2. Block by Block

This organizational method allows the writer to reveal all of his or her points of comparison on one topic first. Then moving onto the next topic, the writer reveals the points of comparison on the second topic, showing how the points of comparison are related to the first topic.

Block by Block Organizational Method

Main Topic 1: 1970s
First point of comparison: *Fashions*
Second point of comparison: *Drugs*
Third point of comparison: *Music*
Main Topic 2: 1990s
First point of comparison: *Fashions*
Second point of comparison: *Drugs*
Third point of comparison: *Music*

3. The Mixed Method

This organizational method allows the writer to use both methods in his or her essay. Depending on the author's purposes, the first third of the essay may use the point by point method while the last third uses the block method. Or perhaps the first half of the essay uses the block by block method, and the final half employs the point by point method. There is no set pattern for mixing the methods.

One way to approach mixing the methods is to consider the amount of information for each point of comparison. For instance, if you have five points of comparison but two of them do not have much information, you could use point by point comparison for the two scanty points of comparison. The amount to which each method is used is entirely at the author's discretion.

Mixing the Methods

Main Topic 1: 1970
  <u>First point</u> of comparison: ***Fashions***
Main Topic 2: 1990
  <u>First point</u> of comparison: ***Fashions***

Main Topic 1: 1970
  <u>Second point</u> of comparison: ***Hairstyles***
Main Topic 2: 1990
  <u>Second point</u> of comparison: ***Hairstyles***

Main Topic 1: 1970
  <u>Third point</u> of comparison: ***Drugs***
  <u>Fourth point</u> of comparison: ***Art and Literature***
  <u>Fifth point</u> of comparison: ***Music***
Main Topic 2: 1990
  <u>Third point</u> of comparison: ***Drugs***
  <u>Fourth point</u> of comparison: ***Art and Literature***
  <u>Fifth point</u> of comparison: ***Music***

Each way of organizing has it advantages and disadvantages. Point by point is best used for shorter essays no longer than five pages or so. Block by block works best for longer works in which switching back and forth between points would become confusing to the reader. Mixed can work well in both long and short essays as long as the points in the comparison/contrast aren't confused. Unfortunately these are not steadfast rules. Some great short comparison/contrast essays, such as Mark Twain's "Two Views of a River," are in block form.

Unless your instructor has told you otherwise, you will have to decide which organizational strategy works best for your topic.

REVIEW—COMPARISON/CONTRAST WRITING

Answer the following questions with 2–3 complete sentences.

1. What are some of the real-world uses for comparison/contrast writing? Give an example of how this style might be used.

2. Briefly explain how a point-by-point organizational strategy is used. Develop an outline using this organization for your own comparison/contrast essay.

3. Briefly explain how the block-by-block strategy works. Use this method to outline an essay of your own.

4. What is the "mixed" organization? How is it similar or different from the two previous methods mentioned above?

5. Look at one of the essays included in this chapter. What is being compared, and which organizational strategy has the author used?

VOCABULARY—COMPARISON/CONTRAST

Words:

1. similarity

2. verification

3. alternate

4. determine

5. cultivation

6. euphoric

7. conscience

8. illiterate

9. bidirectionally

10. conscious

ACTIVITIES

1. Look up the preceding words in your dictionary. Identify the most meaningful definition and the PART OF SPEECH. Now write the words in sentences to show their meanings.

2. Using your dictionary, work with a small group to write a 2–3 paragraph comparison. Try to use all of the vocabulary words from the list on page 97 in your sentences. Make sure that each sentence follows logically from the previous person's.

3. Define the words from above by their context from the readings at the end of the chapter. Are there any other uses or meanings for these words?

WRITING ASSIGNMENTS

1. Write a brief comparison of two or more items. Use the point-by-point, block-by-block, or mixed method to organize your comparison.

Read the following writing samples, then answer the questions that follow with 2–3 complete sentences.

1. What method of comparison is employed in the essay "Computer Literate or Illiterate"? Outline the major topics to support your answer.

2. Compare two of these comparative essays. Choose two or three bases of comparison and draw your own conclusions about them.

3. Identify a topic sentence in one of the comparative essays. Does it appear at the beginning or end of a paragraph? Does it seem to tell you anything, or does it say very little?

Computer Literate or Illiterate

Micheal Lena

There are two types of people in this world, Type A and Type Z. One type is computer literate and the other is computer illiterate. Can you tell who's who?

Type A knows the difference between hardware and software. Hardware is the computer itself, and software consists of the instruments necessary in order for the hardware to do things. Type Z thinks hardware is a combination of Stanley tools, and he or she thinks software is a collection of Tupperware containers.

Type A knows that jellyware is the human being who is telling the hardware what to do, who gives the hardware its data, who writes the software, and who utilizes the output of the hardware. Type Z thinks jellyware is what Welches Grape Jelly is sold in.

Type A knows that the keyboard is used to input data, or to program the computer. Type Z thinks that a keyboard is the board next to the refrigerator where they hang their car keys.

Type A knows that resolution is the number of pixels being viewed on the monitor, 640 by 480 for VGA mode and 1024 by 768 for SVGA mode. Type Z thinks the resolution was fought in 1776.

Type A knows that a byte is an 8 bit binary word used to measure the size of files, hard drives, floppy drives, disks, graphic cards, and RAM. Type Z thinks that a byte is the first thing you do to a hamburger.

Type A knows that a hard drive is the storage for the installed software and files. Type Z thinks a hard drive is that Sunday drive with the kids.

Type A knows the difference between a cold boot and a warm boot. A cold boot is turning on the power switch to the computer, and a warm boot is resetting the computer. Type Z thinks a cold boot is a boot that was left outside all night, and a warm boot is a boot that was left near the heater.

Type A knows that cache is an intelligent buffer located in RAM. Type Z thinks that cache is the amount of money in their pocket at any given time.

Type A knows that a serial port is used for devices that must communicate bidirectionally with the system; such devices include modems, mice, and scanners. Type Z thinks a serial port is a new type of bowl for their Captain Crunch.

Type A knows that an operating system is the computer's command interpreter, and that it has utilities and system files. Type Z thinks the operating system is what you get when you dial O.

Now you know the difference between a computer literate and a computer illiterate. Which type are you? Type A or Type Z?

———————

A Dream versus a Nightmare

Jessica Hammond

The reason for this paper is to compare the two civil rights leaders, Martin Luther King, Jr. and Malcolm X. I will compare their methods of protest, their views of Caucasian Americans, and their different backgrounds. I will provide facts based on speeches given by the two leaders, Martin Luther King, Jr.'s "I Have a Dream" and Malcolm X's "The Ballot or the Bullet." I will explain based on the different comparisons why the methods used in protesting or fighting for a cause are crucial in getting something positive accomplished, and I will also touch on how a person's background can affect opinions and personalities.

Malcolm X was given the name Malcolm Little at birth, but he adopted the last name X to protest his legal status of a slave's descendant. He dropped out of high school and was convicted of burglary at age 21. He taught himself to read in prison by copying the dictionary in longhand. He converted to Islam while in prison. Malcolm X was a devoted Muslim. At one point he joined the radical group called the Black Muslims. He gave his speech "The Ballot or the Bullet" in 1964. He was assassinated in 1965 in New York's Harlem.

Martin Luther King, Jr. was raised in the south. By 1954 he had received national attention for his policy of passive resistance. He was awarded the Nobel Peace Prize in 1964 for his peaceful means of protest. Martin Luther King Jr.'s famous speech, "I Have a Dream" was given on the steps of the Lincoln Memorial in front of 200,000 people in 1963. The people had gathered to demonstrate for civil rights. This was the 100th anniversary of the signing of the Emancipation Proclamation. In 1968 he was assassinated in Memphis, TN.

Malcolm X appears to be a frustrated and violent leader. He wants something to happen now. In his speech he says, "If we don't do something real soon, I think you'll have to agree that we're going to be forced either to use the ballot or the bullet. It's one or the other in 1964" (97). Malcolm feels that violence is the best way to achieve civil rights for blacks. He says,

> It is constitutionally legal to own a shotgun or a rifle. This doesn't mean you're going to get a rifle and form battalions and go out looking for white folks, although you'd be within your rights—I mean, you'd be justified; but that would be illegal and we don't do anything illegal. (98)

Malcolm X is tired of waiting for something to happen. He wants the black race to do something immediately. Malcolm doesn't seem like he wants to give the world a chance. He wants the violence to begin now. He doesn't want to sit around and wait. He wants things done right now. He says, "If a Negro in 1964 has to sit around and wait for some cracker senator to filibuster when it comes to the rights of black people, why, you and I should hang our heads in shame" (99). He doesn't feel that Martin Luther King's method is working. He says, "You talk about a march on Washington in 1963, you haven't seen anything. There's some more going down in '64. And this time they're not going like they went last year. They're not going singing 'We Shall Overcome'" (99). This negativity seems to go on throughout the entire speech. You feel some rage and hate while reading his speech. Maybe that's his point.

Martin Luther King is a peaceful leader. He wants to cash that bad check the black race was given. As stated in his speech, "I Have a Dream":

> It is obvious today that America has defaulted on this promissory note insofar as her citizens of color are concerned. Instead of hon-

oring this sacred obligation, America has given the Negro people
a bad check, a check which has come back marked "insufficient
funds." (93)

It appears that United We Stand is his whole philosophy. He says, ". . .
one day right there in Alabama, little black boys and black girls will be
able to join hands with little white boys and white girls as sisters and
brothers" (95). He wants to use peaceful means to get civil rights for
blacks. As stated in his speech, "We must not allow our creative
protest to degenerate into physical violence. Again and again we must
rise to the majestic heights of meeting physical force with soul force"
(94). Martin Luther King, Jr. wants his people to believe that one day
the world will be a good place. He wants to put across the message
that violence is not the answer. He says, "Let us not seek to satisfy our
thirst for freedom by drinking from the cup of bitterness and hatred":

> I am not unmindful that some of you have come here out of great
> trials and tribulations. Some of you have come fresh from narrow
> jail cells. Some of you have come from areas where your quest for
> freedom left you battered by the storms of persecution and stag-
> gered by the winds of police brutality. You have been the veterans
> of creative suffering. Continue to work with the faith that
> unearned suffering is redemptive. (94)

You know that Martin Luther King, Jr. believes that the suffering will
end, and the world will be united at last. He truly wants America to
become a great nation by joining all the races in harmony.

Malcolm X is disgusted with America. He feels that the black race
are not American citizens at all. At least they aren't being treated that
way. He says, ". . . I don't even consider myself an American. If you and
I were Americans, there'd be no problem" (98). He wants the black

race to realize that they're not being given the same rights as "Those Hunkies that just got off the boat" (98). He goes on to say,

> Sitting at the table doesn't make you a diner, unless you eat some of what's on that plate. Being here in America doesn't make you an American. Being born here in America doesn't make you an American. Why, if birth made you American, you wouldn't need any legislation, you wouldn't need any amendments to the Constitution, you wouldn't be faced with civil-rights filibustering in Washington, D.C., right now. (98)

Malcolm wants his people to believe in themselves and stand up for their rights granted in the signing of the Emancipation Proclamation. But perhaps he is going about it the wrong way. He didn't want to stop long enough to find that "the man" could very well be the ticket he's looking for. Throughout the speech Malcolm refers to the white race in very negative ways. He refers to them as "Hunkies," "cracker," "white political crooks" and "the man." He puts across the message that races don't belong together. He is always talking about them. It's not the human race. It's the black race against the white race. He says,

> And don't let the white man come to you and ask you what you think about what Malcolm says—why, you old Uncle Tom. He would never ask you if he thought you were going to say, "Amen!" No, he is making a Tom out of you. (98)

He feels that the white race doesn't care what the black race has to say or how they feel. He is not willing to give the white people that believe in the civil rights act a chance.

Martin Luther King, Jr. wants the world to live as one. He wants the white and black race to just be the human race. No segregation, no prejudice, and no discrimination. It's plain and simple. He knows that the white race is mixed with people that are prejudiced and people who are not.

> And the marvelous new militancy which has engulfed the Negro community must not lead us to a distrust of all white people; for many of our white brothers, as evidenced by their presence here today, have come to realize that their destiny is tied up with our destiny, and they have come to realize that their freedom is inextricably bound to our freedom. (94)

His famous line, "I Have a Dream," is a perfect saying for what he is trying to put across. He has a dream that one day the white race and the black race will live together as one. That there isn't such a thing as a black water fountain or a black park. Now there are only drinking fountains and parks. No regard to color whatsoever is the point. Let people live together. He wants blacks and whites to sit together at the same table of life. He wants the world to be united.

Malcolm X dropped out of high school and was convicted of burglary at 21 and then sent to prison. This history may have led to his negative outlook on mankind. His faith was probably lost when all he saw was the black race being degraded and disgraced due to the prejudice held by whites. He was raised in Nebraska and this may have exacerbated the problems because the presence of blacks was not very common. He converted to Islam and was a belligerent and radiant leader. He very much believed in the Islamic religion. He truly had the religious austerity and fervor of a faithful Muslim. At one point he belonged to the radical organization called the Black Muslims. He later received his G.E.D. Because of his deep involvement with the fight for civil rights, Malcolm felt as though he had a higher level of education. Because of the situations surrounding Malcolm X's life, you begin to get an understanding of where all of that bitterness and hatred comes from.

Martin Luther King, Jr. was raised in Georgia. He went to Morehouse College, Crozer Theological Seminary, and Boston University. He obviously did very well in school to be able to continue his education to the level that he did. He was awarded the Nobel Peace Prize in 1964 because of his passive resistance policies. He was a Christian, and believed all people are worthy. He brought this nation a long way with his level-headedness. His convictions and sentiment were probably a direct result of his white centered intellect upbringing.

Although both Malcolm X and Martin Luther King, Jr. were both fighting for the same cause, they had very different ways of trying to accomplish this task. Martin Luther King, Jr. was a peaceful leader and Malcolm X was a more violent leader. Both leaders were confident in what they believed in and had faith that civil rights for blacks would someday become a reality. The only difference between the two leaders is just how you get the job done.

CHAPTER EIGHT

PARAGRAPHS AND TOPIC SENTENCES

PARAGRAPHS

Notice when you read anything besides an advertisement that the words come in readable chunks known as paragraphs. Paragraph construction is an important aspect of organization you should become familiar with. Organized information is always easier to understand.

There is no one way to write a paragraph. There is no required word amount or specific length for a paragraph. How then do you know what to put into your paragraph or when to start a new one? Basically, every time you change or introduce ideas, you should use a new paragraph.

Paragraphs allow writers to group major ideas so that clear **organization** can be used. It may be difficult for a reader to understand what you have written if your ideas are jumbled around incoherently, so learn to use paragraphs wisely.

TOPIC SENTENCES

Even though there are not set lengths for paragraphs, there are certain strategies you can employ to help organize the information in your paragraphs.

Paragraphs are very much like miniature versions of an essay. Instead of having a thesis statement which tells the reader what the essay is about, paragraphs have topic sentences which let the reader know what kind of information they are going to read about in each paragraph.

Often times the topic sentence is the first sentence in a paragraph, and the following information elaborates on the idea presented by the topic sentence. However, as in this paragraph, a topic sentence may be the second or third sentence, appearing after some introductory information or example. Nevertheless, the main idea behind a topic sentence is that it lets your reader know the direction your paragraph or paragraphs will be going. A topic sentence lets the reader know what to expect next.

While a topic sentence gives direction to a paragraph, a topic sentence can also introduce two, three, four, or more paragraphs at one time. Consider for example a topic sentence from a comparison/contrast essay comparing two schools according to degrees offered and the quality of education in order to see which school is better. The topic sentence introducing the quality of teaching reads like this:

> While different schools offer different degrees, each school has a high quality of teaching which is based on students' test scores and the level of education held by instructors.

The previous topic sentence then introduces two topics which need elaboration: student's test scores and teachers' level of education. Each topic will require at least its own paragraph. The first topic, students' test scores, could be covered in the same paragraph as the original topic sentence, but the second topic, teachers' level of education, will need its own paragraph.

So topic sentences can introduce the information which will be contained in one paragraph, or they can introduce the information to be contained in a series of paragraphs. Either way, clear topic sentences in your paragraphs are the best way to guide your reader through your essay.

CONCLUDING YOUR PARAGRAPHS

While topic sentences start off your paragraph or paragraphs, it is also good to have a concluding sentence which reinforces the point you've been trying to make. Concluding sentences work well if you've used an example that could be misinterpreted. Concluding sentences work best when your topic sentence has introduced a series or a lengthy, complicated subject, and you may need to remind your reader of your original point.

> At the end of last season, the Giants lost to the Dodgers in a heartbreaking series down in L.A. The first game was won by the Giants in a heroic performance by NL MVP Barry Bonds, and it looked as if the Giants would sweep the series. **However, the Giants pitching staff crumbled in the final game, dashing their pennant hopes.**

The concluding sentence appears in **boldface**. Notice how the final sentence in this paragraph agrees with the topic sentence at the beginning.

TRANSITIONS BETWEEN PARAGRAPHS

While paragraphs can be thought of as self-sufficient blocks of information, it is also important to remember that essays are comprised of paragraphs working together, and the success of the essay depends on how well the paragraphs work together. Think of the different paragraphs in your essay as the players on a baseball team. As in batting, each paragraph has its own opportunity to succeed *in and of itself*. With its topic and concluding sentences, it conveys a certain meaning to a reader which contributes something to the meaning of the essay. However, it is a generally accepted rule of thumb that one player cannot win a game by himself, so without additional contributions from other team mates (i.e., the other paragraphs in the essay) the team will likely lose the game. Thus, players on a baseball team must work together to win ball games, and the more efficient the teamwork, the better the team. The same idea holds true with paragraphs, and it is the **transition** which allows them to work in unison with one another.

A transition is a clause, phrase, or complete sentence that smoothly guides the reader from one major topic to the next. They are related to concluding sentences in that they usually come at the end of a paragraph, but they differ in the sense that, rather than looking back at what was just said, the transition connects the previous paragraph to the next paragraph and major idea.

Let's say, for example, that you have outlined an essay about the importance of teamwork in baseball, and you want to move from a discussion of infield-only plays to infield-outfield plays. Rather than making an abrupt change of topic, the writer in the example below has provided a transitional sentence to take the reader from one topic to the next.

> The double play is the most effective infield defensive play because it can get a pitcher out of an inning in a hurry, and it also allows him to throw fewer pitches. *But an infield who can turn double plays is nothing without a solid outfield to back them up, for not all balls hit are on the ground to an infielder.*
> The outfielders are positioned to field long fly balls or ground balls hit through a hole in the infield. . . .

In this manner, a writer can change major topics smoothly, at times imperceptibly to the reader. This is a hallmark of good writing, because as any traveler can attest, the smoother the ride, the more pleasurable it is!

ARRANGING PARAGRAPHS IN AN ESSAY

One problem that many beginning writers experience is that of disorganization of ideas. When a reader (usually a writing teacher) sees this difficulty, he or she will likely be unable to comprehend the main point of the essay, and because comprehension of the writer's ideas is certainly important, strong organization is a crucial aspect of the writing process.

Poor organization can be illustrated in a simple manner. **Syntax** is the arrangement of words in a sentence, and if the order of words in a sentence is hopelessly jumbled, then a reader will have no clue as to what is being said. For example:

Mary had a little lamb whose fleece was white as snow.

Fleece little Mary was white had as snow lamb a whose.

Say that last sentence out loud. Does it make any sense to you? Of course not! It doesn't make sense because humans must have a sense of order in order to understand an idea. Similarly, your paragraphs must have a logical order to them; if they do not, your reader will be lost.

Arranging paragraphs is done during the outlining step. The outline, as mentioned in Chapter 1, allows a writer to develop major ideas before ever writing a complete sentence; therefore, it is a very important step in the writing process, because it is the skeleton which will become the body of the essay.

But, as most beginning writers often ask, how does one arrange the essay's paragraphs to make the most out of each? Again, this is similar to what a baseball team's manager must do before each game: arrange his players in positions to maximize the ability or potential of each. As a writer, you must decide, and the best way to make informed decisions is to understand the different styles of writing described in this text. If you understand description, narration, persuasion, comparison/contrast, and cause and effect writing strategies, then you will have a better idea of how to organize the major ideas. Also, as is mentioned in Chapter 1, try to read into the assigned essay topic, for this can give you additional clues of how to arrange your major paragraph ideas.

One of the best ways to arrange the paragraphs of an essay, however, is to use the outline and the thesis statement. By definition, a thesis statement is the manager of your office of ideas. If written well, the thesis will tell your reader (and you) where each paragraph should occur in the essay. First, list your major topics. Second, develop 1–2 sentences that incorporate your list of major topics. Third, place these sentences in the introduction of the essay, and then simply follow the lead.

PRACTICE #1

Write paragraphs for the following topic sentences. Be sure to touch on every aspect of the topic in your paragraph as it is written in the topic sentences. Can you write a thesis statement to sum up **all** of the topic sentences?

1. Your college has an excellent English program which involves many different styles of writing, and students will explore ideas about description, narration, and persuasion.

2. It is an excellent place for new or continuing students to get a good education, especially in the fields of computers, business skills, and electronics technology.

3. Graduates tend to be in-demand upon graduation due to the intense program at the college and because of the high quality of instruction.

Now arrange these paragraphs (just arrange their numbers) in a logical order that would make sense if you were writing about this subject. Be prepared to explain why you arranged them the way you did!

_____ **1st paragraph**

_____ **2nd paragraph**

_____ **3rd paragraph**

PRACTICE #2

Match the topic sentences on the left with the paragraphs to the right.

Darts is a challenging game that involves accuracy and strategy.

_____

A. In cricket, players attempt to score each number between 15 and 20, including the bull's eye, and each of these areas must be hit three times. The first to "close" all areas wins the game. In "Around the World," players attempt to hit each number, not including the bull, in numerical order, 1–20. The first one to reach twenty wins this game.

There are many different dart games that can be played with the standard 20-numeral dart board.

_____

B. The foot-fault line, or "hockey," is nearly eight feet from the board, and players must bury darts in an area that is only a few square inches in size. Moreover, a dart player must be able to plan his or her shots to maximize their own scoring advantage, or, in some cases, to "block" other players from scoring areas on the board. These elements together make darts fun and, at times, quite difficult.

Though many games change over time, dart games have remained largely traditional for centuries now.

_____

C. Dart games like "301" date back to the earliest forms of the game. Archers were known to play such games. With all of the high-tech-oriented games of the twentieth century, it's nice to know that this particular sport, not unlike baseball, is largely unchanged, which gives it a certain charm.

Answer the following questions with 2–3 complete sentences.

1. What is the paragraph? How does a writer know when to start a new paragraph?

2. What is the difference between a topic sentence and a concluding sentence? Give an example.

3. What is a transition and why are they important in the study of paragraphs? Can you give an example?

4. Why must a writer be concerned with organization? What is the "right way" to arrange the paragraphs in your essay?

5. Explain how a thesis statement helps a writer to organize his or her essay.

WRITING ASSIGNMENTS

1. Edit an essay or a draft in progress for strong topic sentences and paragraphs.

2. Write an outline for an essay by writing the topic sentences for all paragraphs in a logical organization. When it is time to write, go back and fill in the framework with your own text.

CHAPTER NINE

CAUSE AND EFFECT WRITING

WHAT IS CAUSE AND EFFECT?

Imagine that you are driving down the freeway. Suddenly, brake lights flash in front of you, and you are forced to slow and finally come to a stop. Because you are already late for school, you curse and scream and wonder why this traffic stopped for no apparent reason. As you slowly inch forward, you begin to question the cause for this untimely slow-down.

When you have traveled another few miles, you see the cause of the traffic jam, or what appears to be the cause. You see that a car has rear-ended another, and both drivers are now yelling at one another on the side of the freeway. As the traffic begins to speed up, you smile to yourself, firm in the knowledge that the traffic slowdown was caused by this small fender-bender.

But this may not be the whole story. In a cause and effect relation-ship, a writer must analyze all apparent causes, and, in some cases, even the causes of the causes. Few things in life are so simple that they are caused by one thing; usually, there are complex relationships between actions or events. Yes, the accident may have caused the traffic to slow down, but what was it that caused the first car to run into the second car? Perhaps the whole thing was triggered by a third driver who had slowed to avoid a fourth car, both of which would be miles away. Many times in causal situations there exists a connection between causes that isn't at first apparent.

Cause and effect writing is the analysis of a problem or situation and its apparent causes. Most often, this style of writing is used by sci-entists to explain natural phenomena, by police officers or firefighters to explain a fire or crime, or by students of any number of disciplines (history, environmental science, electronics) who are trying to establish relationships between things. There are several techniques that you should know about this style of writing that will help you to compose stronger cause and effect essays.

WRITING THE CAUSE AND EFFECT ESSAY

The process of cause and effect writing involves several commonly used steps to create the essay.

1. **Choose a topic.** If this sounds obvious to you, remember that carefully choosing a FOCUSED topic is of paramount importance in this writing mode. You must be certain that your topic represents a cause-effect relationship (such as the example given below about violence and the T.V. media). You must also be certain that the major causes can be adequately addressed for the scope of your assignment. If you are writing a very short essay, you should probably choose a simple, very specific subject, but if you have more length to work with, then you may need broader topics, with a number of detailed causes.

2. **Prioritize the Causes.** When composing a cause-effect essay, a writer must consider both **primary** and **secondary** causes. To better understand primary and secondary causes, we offer a plausible example from everyday life. A classic example of cause-effect is the traffic accident.

Let's say that you are on your way to work one morning, and, upon reaching an intersection where the light is green, you are broadsided by a car driven by another person who ran the red light. The effect is a metal-crunching accident, and the primary cause of the accident was the other driver's running of the red light. If we delve deeper into the situation (as the police and insurance companies will undoubtedly want to do), we may discover a plethora of secondary causes. Upon interviewing the driver of the other car, we find out the secondary causes. Notice how these causes can be traced back:

> The driver was late to work, so in an attempt to save some time, he tried to avoid stopping at the intersection.

BUT...

> The only reason he was late in the first place was because he had overslept this morning.

BUT...

The reason he had overslept is because he had been out the previous night celebrating with some friends.

BUT . . .

The only reason he'd been celebrating was because he had just received a nice job promotion.

And so on. As you can see, secondary causes often lead to many other secondary causes, and though the immediate cause of the accident was the man running the red light, there are in fact many other (and equally important) reasons why this tragedy occurred. Your job as a writer is to sift through the many secondary causes and determine their relationships to the effect and their importance. Is it, for example, important to know that this driver who ran the red light who overslept who celebrated the night before was given his job promotion because he had served in the Boy Scouts as a young man? You must know when to draw the line in causal analysis essays.

A possible outline for a sample cause-effect essay is

I.   Introduction and thesis
II.   Primary or best supported cause
      A.   Driver runs the red light
III. Secondary cause(s)
      A.   Driver overslept
      B.   Driver celebrated late
      C.   Driver received promotion

3.   **Organizing your Cause-Effect Essay.** Organization is important in an essay, but it is especially crucial in this rhetorical mode because the way you choose to arrange the major topics will have a direct effect on the main point of the essay. As always, a strong thesis will help you to organize the main points, and you should have a good idea about where your essay is going before you even begin writing it. There are at least two ways to organize your cause-effect essay: 1) focusing on the causes or 2) focusing on the effects. Some writers may even combine both styles.

After you have chosen a manageable topic, decide whether or not your situation deals more with cause or effects. The essay topic will usually dictate this information. Returning to the example from above, it is quite obvious that there are a number of **causes** for the accident, and if this were the topic of your essay, you may write your thesis to reflect your focus on **cause**. However, you may choose to examine what the **effects** of the accident had on the driver who was broadsided. It is your decision, but you should stick to one or the other.

4. **Develop a strong thesis.** As you write your cause-effect essay, in order for it to be meaningful, you must make a point. You may use cause and effect relationships to reveal, demonstrate, or persuade in support of your thesis, the point you're trying to make.

> An accident is not just an "accident." Many times people use this word as a convenient excuse to explain away something that actually could've been prevented. Last year, thousands of Americans were injured in automobile "accidents," but, an analysis of the causes and effects of a typical accident will show that most accidents happen not arbitrarily but for significant reasons that are within our control.

5. **Draw Meaningful Conclusions.** Throughout your essay remember to draw conclusions between your causes and effects. You need to show clearly and continually to your reader how the causes and effects are related to your thesis. If you cannot draw a meaningful conclusion between a cause and the effect that directly supports your thesis, then you might want to drop that cause from your analysis because it has no function in your essay. Whenever possible, try to point out how or why the cause-effect relationship supports the thesis; otherwise, the reader may question the validity of your entire cause-effect analysis. Rule #1 for expository writing: if the rhetoric does not support the thesis, get rid of it!

> Because the driver had stayed up the previous night celebrating his promotion, he knowingly put himself in a position to be tired the next day. It is this conscious decision making that most accident investigators tend to overlook because they are not "primary" causes of the accident. Nevertheless, if this driver had thought ahead, the accident might've been avoided simply by going home an hour or two earlier.

READING REVIEW—CAUSE AND EFFECT

Answer the following questions with 2–3 complete sentences.

1. According to the chapter, what is cause and effect? What is a writer trying to say or do in a cause-effect essay? Give some examples from today's reading.

2. Outline the process of cause-effect writing. What are the important things for the writer to consider when involved in the process of writing these essays?

3. What is the cause-effect relationship that is described in the sample essay about television? Clearly describe the series of events or causes, and be sure to identify the "effect." What is the author's main point?

4. What is the cause-effect relationship expressed in Roth's "Pollution Problem"? Explain the problem and the causes as Roth sees them.

5. Write down some ideas of your own for a cause-effect essay.

VOCABULARY—CAUSE AND EFFECT

Words:

1. focus

2. organization

3. prioritize

4. primary

5. malady

6. clustering

7. counterpart

8. resultant

9. catastrophic

10. remedy

1. Look up the preceding words in your dictionary. Identify the most meaningful definition and the part of speech. Now write the words in sentences to show their meanings.

2. Using your dictionary, work with a small group to write a 2–3 paragraph description or story. Try to use all of the vocabulary words from the list above in your sentences. Make sure that each sentence follows logically from the previous person's.

3. Define the words from above by their context from the readings at the end of the chapter. Are there any other uses or meanings for these words?

WRITING ASSIGNMENTS

1.   Write a cause-effect essay that analyzes a major problem in our society today. Focus on environmental problems, racism, violence, or any other topic that interests you. Show how the problem has evolved from a series of causes, and do any research that is needed.

Read the following writing samples, then answer the questions that follow with 2–3 complete sentences.

1. What is the cause-effect relationship expressed in any of the essays you have read?

2. Compare two of these cause-effect essays. Choose two or three bases of comparison and draw your own conclusions about them.

3. Outline one of these essays and determine a listing of causes. What are the primary causes and what are the secondary causes?

4. In two sentences which use coordination and/or subordination, explain why, according to R.A. Kelsey, our educational system is not functioning well.

Media's Violence

It seems to me that our country is being wracked by a plague of violence. Every day we are bombarded with information about robberies, shootings, rapes, murders; so much so, in fact, that even decent, law-abiding citizens are buying weapons to defend themselves. I contend that America's current violent malady is caused by the news media.

Just look at an average day. Information comes in from all directions, but it seems as if the news media's information always centers around either sex or violence. A typical evening newscast begins with the horrible story of a 15-year-old girl who was murdered and discarded in a school stairwell. The cameras are there of course, rolling their film for all the grisly details, and the viewers, of course, watch with a curious interest that is seemingly innate yet unexplainably perverse (which is the same reason why commuters always slow down to view an auto accident by the side of the freeway). The newspapers are the same way, but they may find it hard to compete with the "live coverage" that their video counterparts are capable of.

Hundreds of millions of TVs are watched each day in this country, and our perception of the level of violence in this country is inaccurate because we think that's all that's going on. Indeed, if we used TV news as a barometer of the country's welfare, we would certainly feel as if this nation were ready for civil war. However, pollsters tell us that violent crime is actually on the decline in America, so why is it that everyone is scared to death out there?

So turn off your damn TV. Pick up a book, or go hang out with a friend. Stop filling your head with a bunch of depressing nonsense. I think that if more people "tuned out" from this programmed societal puke, then perhaps this country could return to the glory it once knew.

———————————

A Perfect World

R. A. "Bear" Kelsey

Have you ever given thought to what a perfect world is? Some would say it would be when man has learned from his mistakes; consequently, there would be no repetition of catastrophic decisions or events. The key word in this scenario is "learn." Which brings me to the issue of our educational system: anyone can see that over the years its primary function has deteriorated tremendously. Let's focus upon some of the reasons why education in this country has taken such a drastic downturn in recent years.

Classroom overcrowding has become a major factor in our schools. Today, class size is mandated to be *no more than 35 students per class* in the state of California. This is simply too high of a number for any teacher. It's obvious that when a teacher has to concentrate on a large number of students that the individual attention given to each of them will decline significantly, and it is this *individual attention* which is crucial to the development of young people. With so many students' needs to address, it becomes impossible (even for the most enthusiastic, energetic, and accomplished teacher) to address the questions of a pupil who does not understand a concept or lesson. Thus, class size has had a profound impact on education.

The lack of qualified instructors has also had a definite effect on the system. Teaching has become a less rewarding career financially; thus, few young adults pursue the occupation. This present situation is the result of low wages offered by school districts and the lack of respect afforded by students and their parents. The saying goes: "Those who cannot do, teach"; nevertheless, you cannot **do** until you are **taught**, and with fewer people wanting to become teachers, the standards are lowered in order to get them into the system. The resultant effect is a pool of unqualified or barely qualified individuals who are unable to teach subjects which they themselves probably do not understand.

Perhaps the root cause of both of these problems is a lack of funding or a lack of commitment to funding the educational system or reforming its organization. With less money available to pay teachers competitive salaries (or too much sunk into worthless bureaucracies), up-to-date instructional material cannot be obtained and the quality of education goes down. Why teach a person how a vacuum tube works when the world is in a transistor technology now? One cannot access the "superhighway" of information with textbook equivalents of Model-T's.

All of these factors, in turn, contribute to the lack of enthusiasm in the students. They realize they're not receiving current information, that their classrooms are packed to the walls, and that they, in some cases, are more knowledgeable than their instructor, so why should they bother? If a child cannot find interest in their schoolwork, they will not want to learn, and instead they may search for more interesting alternatives such as gangs, drugs, or sexual promiscuity.

A remedy to this situation would be to prioritize what our youth really need. The first thing to do would be to enhance the teaching profession. Get rid of that old crap about the "spiritual rewards" of teaching and replace the myth with cold, hard cash. A teacher should be able to earn as much as a doctor. This increase in pay might invite more qualified people into the profession, which would in turn shrink class sizes. Moreover, if teachers were given additional opportunities of professional development as incentives (seminars, child psychology, etc.), they would never stop learning, never become outdated. All of this would lead to more interesting classes and students who want to learn rather than the growing number who today quit because of boredom. Finally, but most important, discipline could be restored. Without it, as we know, there is only chaos, but once schools are put in order, discipline can be more easily enforced. By incorporating these ideas, I'm sure that we can end the growing malady of our educational system.

Pesticide Pollution

Bobby Roth

"To make unclean; contaminate." This is what you will find in Webster's <u>New World Dictionary</u>, as the definition for <u>pollute</u> and this is what we are doing to the world we live in. It is being done mostly due to economics: farmers need to increase production in order to fill our need for more, bigger, faster. Pesticides, however, create contaminated lands and genetic defects, both of which are unacceptable. In 1962 Rachel Carson wrote <u>Silent Spring</u>. It is a fable about a town that dies by its own hand from pesticide pollution. Carson wrote it in an attempt to draw national attention to the damaging effects of chemical pesticides and fertilizers such as Dichloro-Diphenyl-Trichloroethane, otherwise known as DDT. In this essay we will discuss this cause and effect and we will see the destructive relationship between technology and pollution. DDT, a highly effective chemical insecticide, was developed during World War II as an insect repellent to help fight against the malaria carrying mosquitoes in Japan. It worked so well that after the war it was introduced to the farmers and became the answer to pest control for the agricultural industry. The farmer's production went up, due to a decrease in loss of product, and this allowed him to make more money.

As it turned out, however, DDT contaminated the water and soil and entered the food chain. As it progressed through the food chain its concentration levels increased exponentially instead of decreasing and it was then found that these incredibly excessive levels caused severe birth defects and sterility; and sometimes death. DDT was then banned from use in the United States in 1963.

A major factor in this ban was the fable written by Rachel Carson called <u>Silent Spring</u>. It speaks of a beautiful place, "a town in the heart of America where all life seemed to live in harmony with its surroundings" (387). This town was amidst prosperous farms and the area was alive with wildlife until one day "a strange blight crept over the area and everything began to change" (387). There was now a strange stillness about this town. The birds were gone. The hens no longer had chicks. The farmers were unable to raise livestock. The apple trees came into bloom, but there were no bees to pollinate the blossoms to create fruit. The fish died in the streams. The vegetation turned down and withered. "Everywhere was a shadow of death," Carson writes, but the worst part appears at the end of the first chapter:

> The farmers spoke of much illness among their families. In the town the doctors had become more and more puzzled by new kinds of sickness appearing among their patients. There had been several sudden and unexplained deaths, not only among adults but even among children, who would be stricken suddenly while at play and die within a few hours. (387)

It seems "the people had done [this] to themselves" Carson writes.

They "had silenced the rebirth of new life in this stricken world" for

> In the gutters under the eaves and between the shingles of the roofs, a white granular powder still showed a few patches; some weeks before it had fallen like snow upon the roofs and the lawns, the fields and streams. (388)

Technology had provided the town with a pesticide, and the pesticide killed the town. Rachel Carson says it well when she writes, "This imagined tragedy may easily become a stark reality we all shall know," and her attempt to draw attention to the problems of DDT and other chemical pesticides and fertilizers worked. Then President John F. Kennedy ordered a federal investigation, and in 1963 DDT was banned from use in the United States.

Every day we continue to juggle the balance of nature with our technological advances. New pesticides, genetic altering for larger, longer lasting fruits and vegetables, and how many other unknowns are continuously being introduced into our lives every day. Man's needs for more, bigger, faster are constantly trying to be met in this manner. We must stop trying to improve on nature's perfection and instead learn better ways to manage our misuses and wasteful habits; and we will not need more, bigger, faster.

CHAPTER TEN

OTHER FORMS OF PUNCTUATION

LEARNING THE SIGNS

Now that you have finished Chapter 6, you should have a good understanding of how to use commas to add stylistic flair to your writing. Following that same idea, this chapter explores several more forms of punctuation, and, as always, provides some practical tips for using these punctuational forms in your writing to make it better, stronger, faster. The four "other forms" of punctuation in this chapter are the *semicolon*, the *quotation marks*, the *dash*, and the *parenthesis*. These marks of punctuation are as equally important to your writing as the comma and period.

Think of these forms of punctuation as you would any other symbol or sign: know what it means, and do what it tells you. When you see a stop sign, you stop your vehicle because you know two particular things about the sign: (1) its shape, which is octagonal, and its color, red, gives you a well-known symbol that every driver knows the meaning of; and (2) the word "STOP" is a language symbol for the cessation of movement. Punctuation marks, when you thoroughly know them, are like street signs too; they tell you how to read a particular group of words. Get to know the street signs of the language and you will never get lost in it.

Conjunctive Adverbs and the Semicolon

There are three main points to consider when dealing with the semicolon:

1. **The semicolon is a useful little tool for sentence construction.**

Generally speaking, the semicolon joins two independent clauses, and it functions the same as a period or a comma and a coordinating conjunction in this sense. However, a semicolon does not indicate the end of a sentence; moreover, it has a shorter pause than a period. This punctuation mark allows a writer to construct longer sentences without relying too heavily on coordination or subordination.

2. **The semicolon is also used with conjunctive adverbs.**
    Typically, these words function as transitional phrases, and, when used in mid-sentence, they require the use of both a semicolon and a comma. Many a paragraph is made by a good transition; thus, the authors of this book highly recommend their usage! The most common conjunctive adverbs are:

Common Conjunctive Adverbs

consequently	however	then
finally	moreover	therefore
furthermore	nevertheless	thus

   To connect independent clauses with a conjunctive adverb, you must end the first clause with a semicolon, and then follow the conjunctive adverb with a comma.
   Before you begin to experiment with conjunctive adverbs, however, you must learn the meaning of each of these words so that you will know when and where to use them:

CONSEQUENTLY and **THEREFORE** are like saying "as a result of." This transition is usually used, like *because* and *so*, to show a cause-effect relationship.

> The man was forced off the road by Speed Freak Freddy; consequently, his legs were broken when he crashed into the mulberry tree.

or . . .

> I think; therefore, I am.

FURTHERMORE and **MOREOVER** indicate that more related information will follow in the clause that follows the conjunctive adverb.

> The old lady swallowed a fly; moreover, she also swallowed a spider, cat, dog, and horse.

HOWEVER indicates contrasting ideas, much like *but*, *yet*, and *although*.

> I'd love to eat candy all day; however, it makes me break out in hives, so I can't.

These are the most commonly used of the most common conjunctive adverbs. Keep in mind, however, that ***thus*** is usually used like ***therefore*** (in cause-effect situations), and that ***nevertheless*** is synonymous with ***however*** (contrasting situations). Try to mix these words up; do not rely too heavily on just one.

Remember that when conjunctive adverbs join independent clauses, you must use the semicolon before the conjunctive adverb and a comma after it as in the examples above.

If, however, the conjunctive adverb appears in the beginning, the middle, or the end of an independent clause, use commas to set it off.

| Do NOT use conjunctive adverbs in this way! | *The elderly couple; finally, came to their senses.* |
| | NO VERB   NO SUBJECT |

DO use them in this way!	*The elderly couple, finally, came to their senses.*
	The elderly couple came to their senses, finally.
	Finally, the elderly couple came to their senses.

PRACTICE

1. Determine the relationship between the following sentences, and then combine them using a conjunctive adverb. Be sure to use both a semicolon and comma.

    A. The writer of this essay, Cy McClintock, employs many sentences that use coordination. It is interesting to note that he seems to know nothing about either subordination or non-restrictive clauses and phrases!

    _____

    _____

    _____

    _____

    _____

    _____

B. We also discovered in our reading of McClintock's essay, which is entitled "Soo-eee: A Pig-Lover's Paradise," a profound love for the adorable hogs and pigs of the rural South. There is some reference to the distasteful nature of the infamous scene from the movie *Deliverance*.

_____

_____

_____

_____

_____

C. We object to the bucolic and "down-home" language used by this author. We advise any readers of this essay to beware, or better yet, to avoid reading it altogether.

_____

_____

_____

_____

_____

_____

2. Use the following conjunctive adverbs in sentences of your own creation. Be sure to use the appropriate word for the appropriate situation, and do not forget to use the correct punctuation!

1. however

2. consequently

3. therefore

4. moreover

5. thus

WRITING ASSIGNMENTS

1. Write 5-10 sentences that use conjunctive adverbs, and add them to a draft in progress. Try to use all of these words at least once. DO NOT FORGET to use the correct punctuation!

2. Write 5-10 sentences that use a combination of either coordination and a conjunctive adverb or subordination and a conjunctive adverb. Add these sentences to a draft in progress.

The Dash

The two main points of the dash to remember are:

1. **Use the dash to show emphasis.**
   When a person writes, they are transmitting linguistic expressions into a physical manifestation—the printed word upon a page. Many written expressions are used to emulate spoken thoughts, emotions or tones, and the dash can be used for this particular purpose. Generally speaking, the dash is used when a writer wants to emphasize a particular group of words. Related to the non-restrictive phrases from the previous chapter, which are set off by commas, the dash also creates a subordinate word group, except now it is intended to emphasize a particular thought. We might equate a phrase set off by dashes as an interruption, as demonstrated in the following example:

   > The new English teacher—who was a young, good-looking fellow—had a positive influence on all the students in the class.

   In this sentence, a special emphasis has been placed upon the looks and age of the teacher. By setting it off with the dash, the writer is telling a reader that his youth and age should be of some interest to us. This thought is more prominent than even the main action of the sentence—the positive influence he had on students. And often, like all verbal interruptions, a reader is left thinking more about the phrase set off by the dashes.

2. **Use the dash to set off appositives that contain commas.**
   Appositives, set off by commas, rename nouns. With the dash, however, you can place those parenthetical thoughts within another, that is, within the dashes. If you try to set off an appositive that contains commas with commas, then you will create a cryptic confusion of commas. Check out this example:

   > Baseball's biggest problems, free agency, skyrocketing ticket prices, and low morale, are outweighing the hype brought on by a new playoff format.

   Although the appositive is correctly set off with commas, a reader can easily get lost in the rat's nest of commas within the appositive. Be kind to your reader! Use dashes to set off appositives that contain commas:

   > Baseball's biggest problems—free agency, skyrocketing ticket prices, and low morale—are outweighing the hype brought on by a new playoff format.

To appreciate the dash you must understand the philosophy behind its use. You should use it when making parenthetical thoughts, but when a reader sees the dash, he or she will expect a certain emphasis; moreover, you can use dashes to include an appositive word or phrase. Look for it as a reader; use it as a writer!

The Parenthesis

This punctuation mark is also used to express non-essential or parenthetical thoughts, ideas, etc. The only difference now, however, is that the parentheses tell the reader to de-emphasize what is inside them. Contrary to the dashes, which announce a more prominent interruption, the parentheses are more like the whisper or the quiet afterthought:

> Math curriculum (because it seems to have no real-world application) has always been a mystery to me.

The key to using parenthesis (or any other punctuational forms) in your writing is knowing how you would say the same thing. Because writing is an expression of our minds (just as speech is), you must think about how you want to say something. When people speak, we can interpret a great deal from just the nuances of their voice—the tone of voice or the emphasis or de-emphasis that they place on various words—and in order to duplicate those emotions, we must use appropriate punctuation in our writing. Parentheses help to express **de-emphasis**; punctuation tells your reader what you would sound like if you were speaking. Remember that writing is mute and a reader is deaf only if you choose to make it so!

Quotation Marks

Quotation marks are important to study because they have a number of important uses in writing situations. The most common use that writers have for the quotation marks is to cite the words or ideas of another or to indicate a certain type of title. This section will show you not only how to use quotation marks for titles and direct quotations, but also how to cite longer passages that do not use quotation marks, as well as citing quotations within quotations. The appendix for this text gives additional usage rules concerning quotation marks and other punctuation, including the MLA rules for citing sources in an essay. Please be sure to refer to both when necessary.

1. For Titles of Short Works

Quotation marks are used in writing to denote the titles of short works, including essays, short stories, poems, magazine and newspaper articles, chapters in books, and TV or radio episodes. DO NOT USE quotation marks for titles of books, movies, plays, magazines, or newspapers. These titles are underlined or italicized.

> Our English teacher assigned us Poe's short story, "The Imp of the Perverse."

2. For Direct Quotations

When citing the words of another writer, critic, etc., use the quotation marks to enclose the actual words that the person used. The best writers will often bring in the ideas of others to support their own analytical claims:

> Poe says that the perverse is "the unfathomable longing of the soul to vex itself."

Notice that only Poe's words are enclosed in the quotation marks, as well as the ending punctuation. You should not use quotation marks for paraphrased material. Remember, if you do not use quotation marks for direct quotations, you may be accused of PLAGIARISM!

When using quotation marks, be sure to place periods and commas inside the quotation marks (unless you are using the MLA style for in-text citations; see the Appendix.

With MLA style, the cited page number forces the period to the end, OUTSIDE the quotation marks.

> Poe says the perverse is "the unfathomable longing of the soul to vex itself" (35).

Though there are other writing formats, we always advise students to get into the habit of using the MLA format, for it is the accepted essay format in English classes. Be familiar with the various conventions outlined in the Appendix. Then try the following practice.

PRACTICE

1. Rewrite the information indicated below into a single sentence that uses MLA style quotations. Be sure to include the author's name, the quotation itself, and the page number.

- The author is Barbara Ehrenreich.
- The essay is entitled "The Mommy Test."
- Her quotation is this: *The mommy test is an example of discrimination or prejudice.*
- The page number is 66.

_____

_____

_____

_____

- The author is Nathan Glazer.
- The essay is entitled: "Some Modest Proposals for the Improvement of Education."
- The quotation is: *We should disarm our schools.*
- The page number is 136.

_____

_____

_____

_____

- The author is Thomas Sowell.
- His essay is entitled "We're Not Really Equal."
- His quotation is this: *We must define our terms.*
- The page number is 110.

_____

_____

_____

_____

_____

3. For Quotations within Quotations

In some writing situations, you will need to use quotations within other quotations. When this situation arises, use single quotes (or the apostrophe) for the quote within the quote. Say, for example, you want to cite a particular person's quoted reference to a short work:

> My teacher said, "Poe's tone in 'The Imp of the Perverse' is quite gloomy."

Any time you have a double-quotation situation, use the single quotation marks within the regular quotation marks.

4. Quoting Longer Passages

A writer may find it necessary to quote more than just a few lines of poetry, an essay, or a short story, and when your quotation is longer than four type-written lines, you should dispense with the quotation marks and use the indented style. This indented style is used so that a reader does not get lost with a longer quote, perhaps forgetting where it began. The indented style establishes an attractive layout for longer quotations, and it is very clear to the reader when the quotation begins and ends.

To form the indented style quotation, simply indent 10 spaces from the left hand margin. You will not need quotation marks, again, because the indention will indicate to your reader that you are giving a long quotation:

> After rising out of his foxhole on a corpse-strewn beach, Robert Duvall, who plays an arrogant Air Cavalry Colonel, gives Captain Willard his feelings about the war in Vietnam:
>
>> You smell that smell? That gasoline-like smell? That's Napalm. God, I love the smell of Napalm in the morning. It smells like . . . It smells like victory. Yeah, you know, Captain, someday this war's going to end. Someday this war's going to end.
>>
>> —Apocalypse Now

Long quotations like this are usually introduced with a sentence ending in a colon. This introduction, or **transitional clause**, makes your writing flow more smoothly. After using long quotations, provide interpretation of the quotation to show how it relates to your topic sentence.

5. Smooth Transitions with Quotations

When a writer uses quotations, whether brief or lengthy, he or she should always try to smoothly integrate their own words with the words they are quoting. If a writer simply inserts quotation after quotation, without including transitions, the result is an unattractive piece of writing, one that often makes little sense:

> The essay about Nuclear Winter was very frightening. "High yield airbursts will chemically burn the nitrogen in the upper air . . . and these destroy the earth's protective ozone" (423). It was very hard to believe that man could harness so much destructive power: "There seems to be a real possibility of the extinction of the human species" (426).

This writer has not used transitions to make his style smoother. Does it seem to make any sense, or is it difficult to follow for you?

One way to avoid this common pitfall is to remember who wrote those words that you are so judiciously using in your report. Rather than just throwing their words in with your own, introduce their ideas by means of a transitional word or phrase. Determine the quoted writer (or speaker's) tone of voice, and integrate that into your essay. If the author is making a statement, tell your reader that. If the author is pleading, tell your reader that too. Try to read into what the quoted person is saying and how they are saying it. This will make a huge difference when your essay is read:

> The essay, "The Nuclear Winter," was very frightening. Carl Sagan explains that "high yield airbursts will chemically burn the nitrogen in the upper air . . . and this destroys the earth's protective ozone" (423). It was hard to believe that man could harness so much destructive power. Sagan goes on to suggest, "there seems to be a real possibility of the extinction of the human species" (426).

This writer made effective use of transitional phrases, which are underlined above.

The underlined portions of the revised passage indicate transitional words or phrases that ease the reader into the quoted material. In the first case, the author, Carl Sagan, is explaining how ozone is destroyed by nuclear blasts, so the author used the transitional phrase "Sagan explains." In the second case, Sagan is making a suggestion (that the human race might be wiped out), so, appropriately, the author has used the transitional phrase "Sagan goes on to suggest." Use the appropriate word or phrase for whatever the situation demands.

Common Transitional Expressions

the author **states** . . .	the author **feels** . . .
the author **points out** . . .	the author **agrees** . . .
the author **demands** . . .	the author **concludes** . . .

And there are many more, but it is always up to you as the writer to decide which to use. Again, determine what the quoted person is saying, how they are saying it, and then use an appropriate word.

PRACTICE

1. Take the following quotations and put them in sentences that use transitional phrases.

- Person quoted: Robert Duvall
- Quotation: "Charlie don't surf!"

_____

_____

_____

_____

- Person quoted: Marlon Brando (as Colonel Kurtz)
- Quotation: "You are an errand boy, sent by grocery clerks to collect on a bill."

_____

_____

_____

_____

- Person quoted: Harrison Ford (a Captain in Intelligence)
- Quotation: "You are to infiltrate Colonel Kurtz's base in Cambodia, gather whatever information you can, and then terminate the colonel's command."

_____

_____

_____

_____

_____

- Person quoted: Martin Sheen (as Captain Willard)
- Quotation: "Do you know who's in command here, soldier?"

_____

_____

_____

_____

_____

CHAPTER ELEVEN

PERSUASIVE WRITING

THE BENEFITS OF PERSUASION

One of the most used forms of writing is persuasion. It may be used by an individual employee to ask for a raise; it may be used by a student to ask for a particular grade; it may even be used by advertising companies to try to convince would-be customers to purchase a certain product. Whatever the reason, persuasion is a very important aspect of the real world, and understanding how to be a better persuasive writer may help you to "get what you want" out of your life. Indeed, well respected is the attorney who argues persuasively in a courtroom; well revered is the baseball manager who convinces an umpire to reverse a particular call; and highly regarded, especially in American society, is anybody who can get things to go his or her way by using persuasion.

Writing persuasively is easy if you know how to go about doing it, but a piece of persuasive writing must be carefully thought out and crafted, the way an architect plans for a new building. Plans must be laid, and each section of the work must be soundly supported in order for the finished product to work correctly. As a writer, you must organize your ideas very deliberately so that your persuasive essay achieves the maximum potential effect on the reader. Remember, the goal of persuasion is to persuade; if your reader is not convinced, at least to some degree, then your work has failed. Thus, logical and thoughtful organization of ideas is essential to make the persuasion work. Moreover, you must support your claims with, whenever possible, facts, logic, and reason.

GETTING STARTED

To begin your persuasive essay, you must first start with a main idea or a thesis. The thesis should be a persuasive statement that you will support with facts, reasoning, and logic. The thesis must set out to "prove" something to the reader. In his essay on tree-spiking, Edward Abbey attempts to convince his reader that spiking trees is an acceptable form of protest, but in order to do this, he first must introduce the idea that it is our "moral imperative" to fight back against big business and the "three-piece suited gangsters." This is Abbey's premise, and without it, few people (if any) would listen to his radical ideas about tree-spiking.

Similarly, in his essay about global overpopulation, Garrett Hardin starts his persuasive essay with a thesis that there are acceptable solutions (which do not work) and unacceptable solutions (which will work) to population problems. Using this as the basis of his argument, Hardin attempts to find a middle ground: acceptable solutions that will work. The factual information that follows has been introduced, or set up, by the author's premise.

You too must develop a basic thesis for your essay, for your factual support may only make sense with an introduction that prepares the reader for the logic that follows.

USING FACTS, LOGIC, AND REASON

Facts

Once you have established the premise for your essay, then you must provide support for the introduced ideas, and the most effective way to be convincing is to be accurate. This is the method used by courtroom attorneys who win big cases, not by theatrics, but through a thorough understanding of all of the information involved. If an attorney's case is grounded in hard facts, or arguments which are backed by reputable witnesses, then the evidence is usually convincing to a judge or jury. So too must your persuasive essay make effective use of facts, reason, and logic, for without them your arguments become nothing but speculation and hearsay.

Use specific facts to support your basic points. No one can argue with facts, but they must be firmly established facts and not theory. For example, you would not want to base your persuasive essay for settlement on Mars on one quack scientist's opinion that there are rich deposits of oil on that planet. Facts should be well known or at least referenced by another reputable source, and the more reputable the source, the better the choice for use in your essay. If, perhaps Carl Sagan and Stephen Hawking (two very reputable astrophysicists) said there were oil deposits on Mars, then you might have some justification for using that as support for a settlement on Mars. Moreover, if particular studies have been conducted on the Martian oil deposits, and actual numbers produced, then you could cite those numbers as evidence for your claims. But remember: facts, statistics, and numbers are only as strong as their source, so view all sources with some suspicion.

Logic and Reason

Logic is the study of how to arrive at answers through reason, and reason is usually divided into **inductive** and **deductive**.

Inductive Reasoning means to produce generalizations based on collected evidence. This is how scientists produce theories. In 1979, Luis and Walter Alvarez proposed that the dinosaurs went extinct because the earth was bombarded by asteroids which caused a thick layer of dust to cover the planet, blocking the sun's rays so that photosynthesis stopped and temperatures plummeted. What brought the Alvarezes to these generalizations were facts. Before the Alvarezes, most theories on the extinction of dinosaurs did not take into account the fact that not only did the dinosaurs become extinct but so did many other animal and plant species. After analyzing huge amounts of data, paleontologists Jack Sepkoski and Dave Raup discovered that the earth has a history of five mass extinctions, occurring every 26 million years or so. The Cretaceous period, when the dinosaurs ruled and then vanished, occurred during one of earth's mass extinctions. Therefore, the Alvarezes extrapolated that since the earth's ecosystem was stable, the only way such a mass extinction could have occurred was through some extraterrestrial catastrophe.

To further support the theory that something from space hit the earth, scientists around the world have found great increases in iridium in rock deposits around the time the dinosaurs went extinct. Most of earth's iridium arrives through extraterrestrial objects that hit the earth. From the facts, the Alvarezes used inductive reasoning to make a seemingly convincing generalization as to how the dinosaurs died.

Deductive reasoning means to move from the general to a specific case. Aristotle proposed the syllogism as a three-step method of deductive reasoning, including a major premise, a minor premise, and a conclusion.

Major Premise:	All people are mortal.
Minor Premise:	I am a person.
Conclusion:	Therefore, I am mortal.

In the above syllogism, the generalization about people as a group is applied to the individual so that the conclusion states the connection between the two premises, making the general statement "all people are mortal" specific to one person.

If there is a problem with deductive reasoning, it begins with the premises. Consider the following example.

Major Premise:	My grandfather, a mortal man, died laughing.
Minor Premise:	Tom is a mortal man.
Conclusion:	Tom will die laughing.

This is known as a **false syllogism**. The major premise contains a condition, "died laughing," that does not apply to all mortals. Therefore, the conclusion is a false assumption, revealing faulty logic. Just because Tom is a man, it doesn't mean he will die laughing.

ORGANIZING YOUR IDEAS

Perhaps the most unique thing about a persuasive essay is that you may use any of the organizational strategies we've presented in any combination to support the thesis of a persuasive essay. You can combine narration, cause and effect, and compare-contrast writing styles in the persuasive essay. Suppose, for example, you want to argue for the death penalty because it would provide the victims of the crime with a sense of catharsis (see Mencken's "The Penalty of Death"). You could begin by using narration to tell the story of a time a friend was murdered, revealing the issues and feelings family and friends had to face.

Using cause and effect, you could reveal how "getting even" allows people to feel better after having been cheated. Since murder cheats the family out of time with their loved ones and cheats the victim of his or her life, the family's suffering would be directly affected if the murderer received the death penalty.

Then you could use comparison/contrast to compare your ideas with your opponent's ideas regarding the death penalty. Your comparison of ideas would then allow you to refute the opposing side's views against the death penalty, further supporting your position.

ANTICIPATING COUNTER ARGUMENTS

It is also useful for writers of persuasion to anticipate arguments against their case because if you can weaken the opposition, your case will thus be strengthened. If you, for example, are trying to persuade your reader to change something (such as the writer of "Eliminate the Designated Hitter"), then you should try to de-emphasize or cross-examine the opposing arguments. In a courtroom, an attorney may try to weaken the case against his client by ruining the credibility of the witnesses against him; so too should the writer of persuasion attack ideas against him or her.

FOUR THINGS TO REMEMBER ABOUT PERSUASIVE WRITING

1. The same argumentation strategy can be used by the opposing side. Allow yourself to consider both sides. Attacking counterarguments can strengthen your own points.
2. You will never convince everybody your position is right; don't try to save the world.
3. While writing on the subject, your position on the topic may change or reverse completely.
4. The more you read persuasive essays, the more effectively you will be able to compose them.

Persuasion is an important facet of writing. Learning how to write in this style will open more doors for you in our competitive society, and it will allow you to use your mental prowess to get what you want out of life. Hold on firmly to your beliefs and write persuasively!

REVIEW—PERSUASION

Answer the following questions with complete sentences.

1. What is **persuasion**? What are some particular cases when persuasion is used in the "real world"?

2. Briefly explain the importance of **organization** in a persuasive essay. How would you organize a persuasive essay?

3. What is a counter argument? How is it used in persuasive writing, and why is it important to consider when writing?

4. Explain why it is important to use specific facts and clear logic. Give an example of facts and/or logic.

5. What is the author of "Same Old Problem" trying to persuade his reader of? What is the premise of the essay?

6. Write down a few ideas that you have for a persuasive essay. Try to be as specific as possible.

Words:

1. reason

2. articulate

3. refrain

4. violated

5. fallacy

6. controversy

7. specific

8. argumentative

9. perish

10. conviction

ACTIVITIES

1. Look up the preceding words in your dictionary. Identify the most meaningful definition and the part of speech. Now write the words in sentences to show their meanings.

2. Using your dictionary, work with a small group to write a 2–3 paragraph description or story. Try to use all of the vocabulary words from the list above in your sentences. Make sure that each sentence follows logically from the previous person's.

3. Define the words from above by their context from the readings. Are there any other uses or meanings for these words?

WRITING ASSIGNMENTS:

1. Brainstorm or cluster to identify a cause in which you believe. Identify or explain the cause thoroughly. Write a strong thesis statement which clearly expresses your attitude about your cause.

2. Write a persuasive letter to your teacher, asking him or her for a specific grade. Be sure to justify your demands with facts, logic, and reason.

Same Old Problem

Nate Valencia

In the '90s certain things need to be eliminated. From personal feelings, I feel one of the top issues that should perish is elderly drivers. What I mean by elderly is anyone that can no longer fit their skin. Don't get me wrong. I do have grandparents, and I do love them, but they should stay the hell off the road. It takes the average car about ten seconds to go from zero to sixty while it takes the average old person in an average car about thirty minutes to go from zero to sixty; nevertheless, once they get going, it's fun to watch them run stop signs and traffic lights causing major accidents.

Running stop signs and such is usually due to the senior citizen not seeing them, or it may be caused by their co-pilot not seeing them. Sad but true—driving becomes a two person operation: the old man usually drives as the old woman tells him to turn right or left, stop or go. This scares me! Older people tend to stop just as the light turns yellow; consequently, they cause the person behind to slam on his brakes or even rear end them.

Elders are the wisest in the land (experience wise), but they don't know when to throw in the towel. I guess they feel that they can drive by "the force," such as Luke Skywalker did in *Star Wars*, but they can't. An elder in the fast lane doing fifty-five miles per hour is enough to make a person flip them off; moreover, elders who drive side by side on the freeway can "drive" someone to become a freeway shooter.

Personally, I feel this problem can be dealt with quite easily. People of older ages should be tested every year; thus, we can weed out the elders that can no longer hang. We should revoke licenses of anyone that cannot pass the go-cart course at Castle Golf and Games; however, the tests should be recorded on video and aired on national T.V. for our viewing enjoyment. *Rescue 911* look out! I think they would lose their prime time slot to such a show!

All in all, elders should forfeit their licenses the moment their confidence disappears and they become paranoid of everything that moves around them. Another simple solution to this growing problem would be to set up an "Elderly Bus Program" that they could use, perhaps at a low or no-cost fare. This, I think, would help to rid the world of this recurring problem!

Cheaters Cheat Themselves

Blanca E. Romero

In order for some students to stay on top of all their academic classes, they have restored to cheating. Cheating in college has become more and more common, so students feel that the act of cheating once or twice in class is the norm. They feel that by cheating there is no harm done. This act will only make students cheat themselves by undermining the value of their grades and college education. Some students may cheat in classes that are not in their major. Other students cheat because of the pressure and to be able to compete with their peers. Perhaps, if the penalty for getting caught cheating was more severe, fewer students would attempt to cheat. It is unfortunate that some college students resort to cheating in class.

Certainly, Erma Bombeck would agree that students' values have slowly declined. She states "What kind of message are you sending to your children? . . . Don't lie to your mother but you can tell the person at the box office you're big for 11." This type of parenting leads to a declination of moral values within our children. We let them know how important it is to be successful no matter how this success is obtained. Indeed, family may sometimes pressure their children by telling them how much money they have invested, and how important it is for them to graduate with a high grade-point average (GPA). If we continue to cultivate this type of thinking among our children (and students), we can continue to have a serious problem that will ruin their educational future. This declination of moral values is one reason why students cheat in class with no regret.

Many students don't see anything wrong with cheating. Cheating is harmless especially, if cheating is done in only one or two of their classes. "How much harm can I do? Besides, this is not my major" is what numerous students would argue as their defense. I disagree with Michael Moore's counsel to students in his book, *Cheating 101*. He advises students to not cheat in their college major courses, which leads students to cheat in non-required courses. Certainly, Moore is missing the point of cheaters cheating themselves. If students follow Moore's advice and decide to cheat in non-required courses, they are relinquishing the opportunity to learn a new subject. Perhaps, this subject course would be much to their liking, but they will never be able to experience this new knowledge. Furthermore, the subject course could broaden their educational background, which can later assist them with understanding other people's cultures and ideas. How else can students learn about the diversity a college has to offer in which they can later use in life? This act of cheating in a few or some courses is not the way students should view their college education.

Additionally, students will argue that in order to maintain high grades for a high GPA, they have no choice except to cheat. Specifically, a student with a busy lifestyle, may have no time to study. If everyone else in the class is doing well, this student will have no other recourse but to cheat in order to compete with other students. To that student I ask, why are you in college? If you don't have time to study and are unable to maintain high grades, then why put other students in a disadvantage by cheating. Cheaters in class not only sacrifice their chance to learn, but also harm the performance of other students who have taken the time to study to produce high grades. For example, if the course is graded on a statistical curve, the cheaters may skew the curve and hurt students that did not cheat. This is unfair to students in class who have taken the responsibility to study and learn.

Some students continue to cheat because the penalty in cheating is minor. Peggy Miezo, assistant dean of students in the University of Wisconsin, suggests, since the university code changed, numbers in students cheating has increased because the code makes it easier for the faculty to penalize those who violate academic conduct rules. This does not frighten students from violating academic conduct rules. Cheating in some courses is indicative of mild penalization in the University of Wisconsin. If a college has a high number of students who cheat, it undermines the integrity of the school. Therefore, the value of the college's grades have deteriorated. I feel that if a student cheats during an exam and the instructor catches the student in this act (of cheating) and has evidence to support such an act, then the university has the responsibility of taking action.

The punishment must make cheating a less attractive option for students. For example, the university can fail the student from the course for cheating as a first time offense. For the second time offense, the university expels the student from school. Students need to understand that they are in college to learn and that cheating is not acceptable. Colleges must not allow cheating to continue. The college is responsible for the students to learn, not for policing each student. As mentioned earlier, allowing cheaters to cheat and penalizing them mildly will condone the act of cheating. If colleges initiate more severe punishment for breaking academic conduct rules, by failing and expelling students for cheating as their punishment, conceivably students will think twice before they cheat.

Cheaters cheat for different reasons, but the outcome of their lie is dishonesty to themselves. As long as students continue to be in agreement with Moore's advice, we will continue to have a growing number of students who will cheat because they think it is harmless. Students need to learn that cheating in class is to cheat yourself from the diversity a college education has to offer. They run the risk of getting caught cheating, and also place students who don't cheat at a disadvantage. A greater penalty for cheating would make students think twice about their dishonesty to themselves.

Eliminate the Designated Hitter

Baseball is a game of tradition; the rules, dimensions, and scoring have remained consistent for the better part of a century. But the designated hitter rule (DH) has forever changed the game of baseball because it actually removes one fascinating and unique aspect of the game—players must play both offense and defense, and they must have above average ability at both to be successful.

Unlike other popular sports like basketball and football, which have free substitution and "specialty" players, baseball requires a player to bat and field, and if the player is removed, he stays out of the remainder of the game. This places an incredible emphasis on the <u>individual</u> ability of a player, for they must be able to go nine innings (usually about three hours) and maintain a level of consistency in the field and at the plate. In a sense, traditional baseball rules, by their simple implementation, create a more rounded player—a man who can do it all. This is akin to the modern university student: an individual who is accomplished at many skills: the arts, sciences, letters, etc. According to Castiglione, an Italian Renaissance writer, the all-around man was better and more refined than the simple-minded brute who was only accomplished at one thing.

The DH rule, which was implemented in the 1973 season in the American League, allows for the manager of each team to substitute a hitter into the lineup in place of the pitcher. This DH does not take a defensive position when his team is in the field; rather, he simply bats, and then he waits in the dugout until his next at bat. The existing practice is to substitute the DH in the batting lineup for the pitcher, for most pitchers are not good hitters. Thus, proponents of the DH argue, the game has become more "pure." Instead of having an automatic out in the lineup, the DH allows one more "real batter," or a person who has a better chance of creating some offense. This, in turn, should lead to more runs per game, which will then lead to more interest in the game itself.

But while the designated hitter may add offense to the game (which it has, according to a comparison of statistics between the National League—no DH—and the American League), the game of baseball has metamorphosized into a different sport, and this change seems to be for the worse. The DH has created a system that no longer can boast the "superplayer"; moreover, the change has also altered the elite status always associated with baseball players, for the game has sunk down to the level of other, newer American favorites like basketball and football.

The game of baseball, for nearly eighty years, required all players to play a position in the field and to bat. Due to the nature of the game, however, pitching has been always the major focus of defense, because a pitcher (with his catcher) handles the ball at all times. This aspect of the game gives pitchers a lot of control and influence on the game; indeed, if a pitcher is dominating enough, he might get by without any fielders behind him. As a result, teams, in order to succeed, need good pitching, and at all levels—from little leagues on up through the minors and the pros—pitching development is of paramount importance. This is one of the advantages of the DH rule: with no time needed for batting practice, a pitcher can spend more time working on his form, pitches, moves to first, etc. But who's to say that an individual who is gifted enough to pitch for a major league team is simultaneously incapable of being just as skilled with a bat? This seems to me a flaw in logic.

In the youth leagues, as any coach can attest, the most athletic and coordinated kids are made pitchers; it is also sort of a general rule of thumb that these kids are also the best hitters. It makes sense, really, because the best baseball players must have speed, agility, hand-eye-coordination, and strength, and the kids who have these gifts are always placed in the most important positions, on offense and defense. The average champion in a little league has four or five "good" players, but there are always at least a couple who are "outstanding players," and these are the guys who pitch, catch, and bat at the top of the order. These players will win or lose the game, depending on the kind of day they have together, and it is important to remember that they are skilled at **both** offense and defense. These are also the players who may one day find themselves in high school leagues, and, if they are really good, the minor or major leagues.

But when these players reach the high school level, they also get into a DH system. Nearly all high schools now use the DH, so those players who were once excellent pitchers and fielders now become just pitchers. Never mind that an excellent shortstop/hitter is an even better shortstop/hitter when he graduates. The pitcher is forced to surrender the bat in favor of the rubber, or he must make a choice to play another defensive position. This is like working the muscles in your legs and back but letting those in your arms and chest atrophy. What could have been a beautiful organism now looks strange or ugly. The DH rule is responsible for creating such lopsided creatures as "the starter," "the closer," "the short reliever," (men who pitch a few innings then rest for a few days, but who cannot hit a beach ball) and the DH himself, a man who can hit but who plays no defensive position. Gone are the heroes like Cy Young, Ty Cobb, Babe Ruth, Don Larsen, Willie Mays. These supermen have been replaced by the likes of Candy Maldonado, Randy Myers, and Chili Davis.

Which leads to the point that baseball has become a changed being. With too much expansion, multimillion dollar salary wars, a half-dozen strikes in the past twenty years, and a watered down pool of talent, baseball has slumped into the ho-hum status in the past two decades. With the new playoff format, too, baseball has come to resemble football and basketball more and more, and this is perhaps the biggest tragedy, for baseball once was, literally, in a league of its own. Though baseball rules were altered on occasion (the height of the mound, for example, was raised and then lowered again), the game was "pure" for many decades. Only since the American League's implementation of the DH rule have fans seen the most dramatic changes in the game, which have included such non-favorites as unlimited free agency, the addition of four new franchises, re-alignment of divisions, and now, wildcard playoff spots for those teams who have the next best record behind the first place finishers. No longer the beautiful sport that Castiglione's Courtier might've appreciated, baseball is now trying to fit in with a changing American society—it's becoming specified, made-to-order.

I say eliminate the designated hitter. Give the bat back to the pitchers and let them hit. Hell, teach them to hit. The best way to get America interested in baseball again is not revenue sharing or free agency or expansion; we need to have more supermen. Give us back the beauty, the grace, the eloquence, and the stamina of the baseball player of old, and then we will have returned to what is known as "baseball purity" or "tradition."

Baseball Is Better with Designated Hitter

Lowell Hickey

Baseball is a better, more exciting sport with the designated hitter than without it. The "designated hitter" rule, adopted by the American League in 1973, allows another player to be substituted for the pitcher in a team's offensive lineup. This player participates in the game only on offense. Opponents of the DH—as the designated hitter is commonly known—like to call themselves baseball "purist." In reality, they are baseball cavemen. Baseball is a marvelous sport without the DH rule; it is even better with it. No sport is so perfect that it cannot be improved. The original rules of baseball, for example, allowed a defensive player to throw the ball at a runner. If hit by the thrown ball, the runner was "out." Of course, he might also be out cold. When the rule was changed so that the ball had to be thrown to the base, there undoubtedly were 19th Century "purists" who objected.

The designated hitter rule takes into account the unique nature of the game. Baseball is a team sport, but with many individual sport characteristics. Roger Clemens pitching to Ken Griffey, Jr., is as man-to-man as a sport can be. It rates right there with Ali vs. Frazier or Borg vs. McEnroe. It is not until the ball is hit, or missed, that the team aspect of baseball comes into play. Because of the individual nature of the game, the pitcher is the most important player on the field. He is so important, in fact, that a person with pitching talent can earn a spot on a major league roster regardless of his hitting ability, or lack thereof. And that goes for the National League where pitchers are required to bat. (Notice it says required to "bat"; they are not required to "hit.") Requiring a pitcher to come to the plate on offense does not make for "complete" ballplayers, as the self-proclaimed "purists" claim. It merely gives the poor guy an opportunity to embarrass himself three or four times a game and that's what happens more often than not.

It is true that a few pitchers are decent hitters. Although hitting and pitching have no correlation, most major league pitchers were probably good hitters in high school or youth baseball because they are better-than-average athletes. But the major leagues is something else altogether. Hitting on the professional level is extremely difficult for even an exceptional athlete, as Michael Jordan discovered in 1994. Also, because a pitcher can only pitch once every five days, he bats very infrequently compared to his teammates and thus cannot maintain the sharpness that hitting requires. A customer paying $15 or $20 a ticket to see a major league baseball game deserves to see a legitimate major league hitter at the plate 100 percent of the time. In the National League, the fan sees an imposter at the plate 11 percent of the time, unless there's a pinch hitter.

Opponents of the designated hitter rule argue that there is more strategy involved in the National League because a manager must decide whether or not to pinch hit for a pitcher in the middle or late innings of a close game. Even if that were true, it would not outweigh the negatives of having to watch pitchers try to hit. But in fact, there is more strategy involved in the American League. The decision of whether or not to pinch hit for the starting pitcher may come up once a game. But the pitchers spot in the batting order, which is usually the ninth spot, comes around three, four or five times a game and that's when the American League manager has more options than his National League counterpart. In the first six innings of a game, a pitcher who is throwing effectively is unlikely to be lifted for a pinch hitter regardless of the offensive situation. He is too valuable on defense. And because of the pitcher's limited offensive ability, the manager's strategical options are reduced. If there is one out with a man on first and the pitcher is up, everyone in the park knows he will bunt. In the American League, by having a legitimate offensive player at the plate instead of a pitcher, the manager could call for a steal or a hit-and-run; he could have the batter hit away or bunt; the options are numerous.

There are other reasons that favor the designated hitter rule. There is more offense in the American League because the pitcher doesn't hit. American League pitchers must face nine legitimate hitters, not eight and an "automatic out." There are less strikeouts with the designated hitter. A pitcher who is throwing effectively does not have to come out of the game for a pinch hitter. An established superstar sometimes can prolong his career several years by becoming a designated hitter. All those factors enhance the fans' enjoyment of the game.

What it all boils down to is this: major league pitchers are there because they can pitch. They didn't have to hit a lick to get where they are. So, don't ask them to try to do something they're not paid to do. It's like asking Joe Montana to play linebacker on goal line defense.

CHAPTER TWELVE

READING AND PROOFREADING

Reading is a skill that, though threatened by video mediums such as the television and the motion picture, is still very important in our society today. In the United States alone, over 40 million people are functionally illiterate, which means that their ability to read is so low that they are simply unable to perform many functions that we take for granted—reading the phone book, street signs, maps, etc. Much of our daily lives involves reading, and so it is always a benefit to have good reading skills. Moreover, the ability to read well also enables a person to write better prose of his or her own, so reading skills are related to writing skills. We, naturally, like to emphasize this aspect of reading!

Notetaking

Most people tend to be passive readers; that is, they expect to just sit back and let their brains absorb all that the eyes see. However, as most scholars will tell you, this is not an effective method of reading and retaining the information. You see, a piece of writing is not a television program where very little brain power is required. When we read, we must learn to be active participants in what is going on, and the more we participate, the more we will understand. This is why reading has not succumbed to the video generation; without a doubt it is the stronger of the two because it stimulates mental activity rather than depressing it.

For everyday reading, we usually need only read the material once—a bill, a newspaper or magazine article, etc.—but when we read more scholarly material, it is helpful to read the piece twice or even three times. Think of reading by this analogy: Say you visited Disneyland as a child. Your first visit was undoubtedly exciting and interesting, but over time the details of each ride and each character have become lost in a swirling confusion of colorful memories. If you were to visit Disneyland now, as an adult, your perception of the place would undoubtedly be different, and certainly more clear to you. So it is with reading. The more times we can visit a particular piece of writing, the better chance we will have of remembering the details and nuances of it.

But we can hear you screaming now, as many a teacher has screamed throughout a graduate career in literature: Who has the time to read a book, essay, or short story through more than once? And the answer to that, generally, is no one. In a perfect world, we could take all the time we needed to read, and we would read books through time and again, getting to know the characters, plots, etc. College courses would not be 10-week quarters, but year long courses that allowed us to read at our own pace and explore the ideas expressed in the literature more thoroughly. Wake up, Dorothy! It's only a dream. . . .

The simple fact is that we do not have all the time to read, and this is one of the reasons for the popularity of TV and movies: they are fast, easy to comprehend, and involve little or no thinking. However, for those who are interested in further self-development, there is a way to read something once through and still remember it as if you'd read it twice. This method is what is called **reader participation** or **annotation**.

The idea is certainly not a new one, for scholars have been writing notes to themselves since time began; however, for many students, writing in your book is something that teachers have taught as a no-no since time began, especially if you attended a public school, where books are recycled year after year. But we say break those chains that bind you! Emancipate yourself! Write in the margins, on the cover, on the text itself! It's your book now, so do as you please; do as you must!

The concept of notetaking is simple: as you read, simply write down notes to yourself (usually the margin is the best place for notes). We have found that one of the best things to write in the book is plot summary or major ideas. As you read each paragraph, try to determine the main action or the main idea, and then, to the side of the text, scribble in some kind of note that will help you to remember what the author is saying. Take a look at the following example of annotation, taken from Edgar Allan Poe's "The Philosophy of Composition":

The author should always keep in mind the "unity of effect" when he writes a work. This is to say that he or she should try to impart some sort of impression on the reader. Poe also mentions that a work of literature should be able to be finished in one setting. He notes that *Paradise Lost*, though written by a talented John Milton, was too lengthy and therefore lacking in the unity of effect.

Notice how the reader has attempted to make some sense of Poe's ideas through notes written in the margin. This is the action that allows a reader to read something twice while only reading it once. The notes will service as a brief outline of the piece you have read, so that you can go back through and review the major ideas at any time following your initial reading. Careful notetaking will add a little time to your first reading, but by "communicating with the text," you will not only be able to go back and look over the major ideas, but you will have reinforced them in your mind too. You might even be able to take your notes and transfer them to another piece of paper in an outline form (time permitting, of course). See Figure 12–1.

Figure 12–1 An Outline of Major Ideas in "Philosophy of Comp."

 I. Introduction
   A. other writers
   B. building from the denouement
   C. working towards an "effect"

 II. Designing the work
   A. Choose an effect
   B. select the length of the work
   C. select the refrain

 III. The creation of "The Raven"

READING LITERATURE

Major ideas are important in the study of essays like "The Philosophy of Composition," but when we read literature, we must take other concepts into consideration. These **literary terms** are important to the study of all literature, however, because they help a reader define how the work is written, how a story is told, who the characters are, etc. It may be helpful for a reader to write notes to herself on these literary terms too, but first you must get a basic understanding of the terms themselves.

Plot

The **plot** of any piece of literature is the structure of its action. Plot is defined as action, but it is related closely to **characterization** because the actions that form the plot are performed by the characters of the work. However, the plot is generally viewed as the sequence of actions that leads from the beginning of the work to the end.

Usually, a plot can be described by **Freytag's Pyramid**, which was created by a nineteenth century critic by the same name. Freytag believed that a typical plot followed a specific pattern that could be drawn as a simple pyramid (see Figure 12–2), and according to this pattern, three main actions could be plotted—**rising action**, **climax**, and **falling action**. Though Freytag intended his pyramid for dramas, the pattern has been used to describe many works of short story or novel form, and they echo

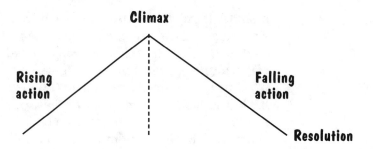

Figure 12–2 Freytag's Pyramid

the Aristotelian model of a unified plot, which says a story must have a beginning, a middle, and an end. Again, see Figure 12–2.

Characterization

The characters in a piece of literature, as mentioned above, perform the sequence of actions that creates the plot. The main character in a work is called the **protagonist**, and usually this person is the focus of much of the plot's action. If the protagonist has a person opposing them in the story (such as Superman versus Lex Luthor, or The Joker versus Batman), we would call that person the **antagonist**. Many great works of fiction have used this model of characterization.

There will also be any number of minor characters in a given piece of literature. Minor characters perform different functions, but generally they serve the protagonist or antagonist in some way, or they contribute a part to the overall action of the plot. Some works, like Joseph Heller's *Catch-22*, have dozens of minor characters, while others have only a handful, as in Salinger's *Catcher in the Rye*. Minor characters should perform some function, or we might wonder why the author has included them at all!

Point of View

The point of view is the perspective through which the story is told. Actions happen, and characters exist, but all of this must somehow be conveyed to a reader. Just as you see things through your eyes each day, so may somebody else see the same things but differently. If two cars collide at an intersection, for example, a police officer might hear two totally different accounts of the same accident. One driver insists his light was green, while the other maintains the same. Thus the same action has occurred, but if each driver tells the story the way it was filtered through their respective brain, then the story becomes changed—depending upon who tells it.

In literature, there are three particular point of view forms:

1. First Person Point of View
2. Second Person Point of View
3. Third Person Point of View
   A. Limited
   B. Omniscient

First Person Point of View is told from the "I" position. The narrator, who is usually a character in the story being told, filters the facts and events as he or she sees them, and then passes them on to you. This may be compared to a person recounting an event to you just after it has happened. Huckleberry Finn, for example, is both teller and protagonist of his story *The Adventures of Huckleberry Finn.* and everything that happens in the story happens through him. Thus, too, we never leave Huck Finn; if we lose him, we lose the whole story, literally.

Second Person Point of View is not so common in literature, but it involves a narrator who assumes to be very close to you, the reader. Not unlike the first person above, the person who tells a story in second person refers to him or herself as "I," but will also refer to you as "you," like a friend or relative. T.S. Eliot's "The Love Song of J. Alfred Prufrock" is a good example of second person point of view, for it begins: "Let us go then, you and I."

Third Person Omniscient Point of View is a commonly used convention that gives the narrator god-like knowledge of everything going on in the story: This narrator can read minds at will, move forward or backward in time or space, and tell (or not tell) any information that he or she wants to. The omniscient narrator is not a character within the story but is able to view everything, like an eagle flying high above. A good example of a third person omniscient narrator is Homer's *Odyssey*, in which the narrator jumps back and forth between Ulysses, the gods, Penelope, etc.

The Third Person Limited is related to the first person because we tend to see the story from one person's perspective, except in this case, that character is not actively telling the story. It's almost as if we are perched upon that person's shoulder for the duration of the work, and we see what they see and feel what they feel, yet we can go elsewhere if we need to. This form was used a great deal by Henry James, Stephen Crane, and William Faulkner.

Setting

The **setting** defines the actual locale, or historical time, in which a story takes place. Setting may be a particular place (such as Hawthorne's Salem in *The Scarlet Letter*), or it may be a very general, fictitious place (such as Tolkein's Middle Earth or *Star Wars* galaxy of "far, far away"). The setting of a work may influence its characters' actions, or it may dictate the tone of a work too (see **tone**).

Tone

Tone is generally defined as the author's attitude about the subject, characters, plot, etc. Tone is used primarily in non-fiction writing, but it does pervade fiction too. Tone can be equated with the familiar phrase "tone of voice," or you can think of it as the "mood" that the speaker is in as he or she tells the story or writes the essay.

For example, consider yourself when you are angry. In such situations, you tend to speak in a manner that reflects your anger, and the tone of your voice would be much different than if you were happy or joyful. These tones, when we can **hear** them, give us signals about what frame of mind a person is in, and if we know how they are thinking, then we can respond in an appropriate manner, or expect them to speak in a particular way. Thus we do not expect angry speakers to use jokes; nor do we expect catechism from a flippant speaker.

Tone can be used by a writer to express indignation, sadness, jubilance, confusion, fear, or any other emotion that human beings are capable of expressing.

> Wild, driving clouds full of rain raced madly across the night sky. Doors were clattering open and shut with the force of the wind as it blew across the desolate prairie farm. Ma and I ran into the storm cellar to escape the approaching tornado. We could not save the defenseless chickens.

This example uses descriptive adjectives which all evoke a certain mood in a reader. What is the writer's tone in this passage?

Remember, these are just some of the literary terms that you should look for when you read. As a rule of thumb, you should always be able to determine plot (or main idea), major and minor characters, setting, point of view, and tone. If you have a good understanding of how these things work in the piece you are reading, then you will undoubtedly have a firm understanding of the piece itself. Remember to write notes in the margins concerning these conventions, or, if it's easier, in a notebook or in an accompanying journal book. The more ways you can look at a story, the more sides you see it from, and that will help make its "meaning," whatever that meaning is, more clear to you as the reader!

PROOFREADING

Proofreading is of paramount importance in writing because it is the safety net that can save the writer from careless disasters. As the last step in the writing process, proofreading allows a writer to correct mechanical or usage errors, or to alter the entire piece of writing. This section will teach you some helpful proofreading habits so that you may keep your final product error-free. Do not take proofreading lightly! It is just as important, if not more so, than the actual writing itself.

Proofreading Checklist

One of the following pages you will find eight easy-to-follow steps for better proofreading. Treat this section as you would a troubleshooting guide; your piece of equipment (or writing) cannot work without this essential series of tests. More importantly, however, is for you to develop a systematic habit of proofreading and the ability to recognize what is "correct" and what is not. Before you know it, proofreading will be second nature to you and your writing process.

1. Check the validity of your response.

Check to make sure that you have adequately addressed each aspect of the assigned topic. Have you answered all of the questions asked of you? Have you written according to the conventions of the rhetorical mode you have chosen? In other words, have you communicated your ideas as clearly as possible? We list this step first because unless your meaning is clear, the mechanics won't matter one bit, right or wrong.

Below you will find a number of practice assignments. Try to determine how the writer could have better addressed the assigned topic. What details are missing or overdone?

Topic #1—Description: Describe your favorite place

My favorite place is a small park just north of Santa Cruz called Butano State Park. It is about 35 miles north of Santa Cruz but about 20 miles south of Half Moon Bay. I have visited there many times, but my most favorite visit was when I went with my Environmental Science class. We had a fabulous time. We spent most of the first night telling ghost stories and singing songs, and we got to know one another too. The next day we made a huge breakfast over the campfire and then took a long walk up to Ano Nuevo Overlook. The view was beautiful—you could see all the way down to the coast. I will never forget that trip.

2. Choose your verbs wisely

Have you used correct verb forms and have you kept the verb tenses consistent? If you do not normally have trouble with verbs, you may hurry through this step, but if you do normally have trouble with verbs, you should spend the majority of your time getting them right. Follow these three easy steps:

1. First determine when the main action of the writing is taking place. The verb tense can usually be determined by reading the first sentence of your essay. If it has already occurred and is finished, use the simple past tense (for main verbs and helping verbs). If you are describing habitual actions or facts, use the simple present tense. If the action will happen in the future, use the future tense. Be sure to keep your verbs consistent throughout because when you shift back and forth, your reader will get lost in time, literally!

2. Look for key verb indicators such as helping verbs (such as *have* or *to be*) and -ing endings. These indicators should be looked at closely, for many students make errors in verbal phrases that make up the passive, perfect, and progressive constructions.

3. Use your dictionary to determine if you have used the correct verb form. These references will help you with irregular verbs that have unique forms in the simple past or past participle.

Please refer to Chapter 2 for more specific information about verb usage.

PRACTICE

Proofread the following paragraph and correct errors in verb tense, agreement, or form.

> The toga party was a complete success. It all began at around 6:30 last night when Freddy arrives with his tie-dyed sheet wrapped loosely around his waist. My roommates and I was not surprised when Freddy says, "Hey, let's TOGA!" Before too long, we were all sported sheets, and when some guy from down the street had showed up with a copy of "Louie, Louie," the party got underway for real. I remembered very little of what happened after that because we were all so busy dancing, sang songs, and commented upon each other's togas. And today, the house was a mess.

3. Solidify your sentence structure.

In this step, you should look at the construction of each of the sentences in your essay. Follow the sentences from the capital letters that mark the beginning of the sentence all the way through to the ending punctuation. In particular, look closely for errors with fragments and run-on sentences. You can catch the comma splices in the next step.

To spot fragments, look for sentences that begin with subordinating conjunctions such as *since*, *as*, *because*, etc. If you do not follow the clauses that begin with these words with a comma, you may have a fragment, especially if you've used a period instead. Also, look for unusually short sentences. Check to be sure that all sentences have both a subject and a complete predicate (verb). If possible, attach the fragment to another adjacent sentence.

To find run-ons, look for exceedingly long sentences. Run-ons usually occur when the writer forgets the punctuation, and if you have a sentence that runs on for four or five lines, there is a strong possibility that you have omitted some form of punctuation.

PRACTICE

Proofread the following paragraphs and correct errors in sentence structuring. Look for both fragments and run-on sentences.

Few people can dispute the genius of James Marshall Hendrix. Also known as Jimi. He captivated the rock industry in 1967 with his incredible talent for playing the electric guitar. When he exploded on the scene. He performed at the Monterey Pop Festival he was the headlining act who burned his guitar before an audience who had never seen such things done on stage before. As he squirted lighter fluid into the burning pyre and his band played the bass and drums behind him. He sang "Let me stand next to your fire." At that moment a legend of rock and roll was born he never looked back until he died of a drug over-dose in 1970 he was all of 27 years old.

4. Control your use of commas.

View all forms of punctuation with suspicion, but especially the commas. Now look for comma splices (independent clauses joined by a comma). Correct the error by one of three methods:

1.   Add a coordinating conjunction.
2.   Change the comma to a period.
3.   Change the comma to a semicolon.

You must also check now for correct usage of both coordination and subordination. Look for independent clauses joined by FANBOYS. Have you placed a comma before the conjunction? Also check to see that you have used commas before only **coordinating** conjunctions; that is, conjunctions that join independent clauses and not just words or compound verbs.

For subordination, look for sentences beginning with the common subordinating conjunctions (*as*, *because*, *if*, *since*, etc.). You should know that these words create dependent clauses that must be followed by a comma. Have you remembered these commas? Remember also that when these conjunctions are used within a sentence, they do not need a comma before them, unlike the coordinating conjunctions!

To help yourself find comma errors, remember this simple tip: If you cannot justify the use of a particular comma by one of the five rules listed below, then chances are it is unnecessary and should be removed. Here are the five rules for comma use:

1.   Use a comma with coordinating conjunctions to join independent clauses.

Team USA has advanced to the second round, <u>and</u> they have silenced their international critics in the process.

2. Use a comma following dependent clauses that begin with a subordinating conjunction or after an introductory phrase.

> <u>Although</u> they were not expected to a win a game, the Cameroons fought like true competitors.

3. Use two commas to set off non-restrictive elements such as the appositive and the adjective clause.

> Cameroon's brave goalkeeper, <u>J. A. Bells</u>, said "I don't care if we don't get paid."

4. Use a comma between three or more items in a series. The last comma, the one that precedes the conjunction, is optional.

> A goalkeeper needs superior skill in kicking, blocking, and throwing in order to compete in the World Cup.

5. Use commas correctly when writing dates, addresses, etc.

> The first World Cup game at Stanford University in Palo Alto, California was played on June 20, 1994.

If you cannot cite one of the above rules for a particular comma, then get rid of it.

PRACTICE

Edit the following paragraphs and correct errors in comma placement. Look for coordination, subordination, non-restrictive elements, and the comma splice.

> On March, 24, 1989, the Exxon tanker Valdez ran aground on a well-marked reef in Prince William Sound, Alaska. Although initial reports of the spill were horrifying Americans did not get the real shock until the film footage came rolling in. The news that night showed a sticky black slick and we watched helplessly as the corpses of wildlife were hauled out and stacked in piles. We were being told that the skipper of the ship Captain Hazelwood was legally drunk, it had been reported that the third mate had been steering the ship at the time of the accident. It was truly an incredible event in American history.

5. Coordinate conjunctive adverbs and semicolons.

Check your essay through for any use of conjunctive adverbs such as *however, consequently, therefore*, etc. If you find one, determine its position and function in the sentence. Does it join independent clauses of equal rank? If so, it should be preceded by a semicolon and followed by a comma. If the conjunctive adverb begins a sentence, it should be followed by a comma, and if it is used in mid-sentence, it should be set off with two commas, the way you would a non-restrictive phrase.

Check other semicolons to see that they are used to join independent clauses.

PRACTICE

Edit the following paragraph for errors in conjunctive adverbs and the use of the semicolon.

> <u>Ecotopia</u>, by Ernest Callenbach, is an interesting view of the not-so-distant future of environmental policy in America; consequently, it is often criticized as being too fantastic or dream like. These critics point out that Callenbach's ideas; however laudable they may seem, simply are not feasible in the real world. But one cannot ignore the grand eloquence of a country devoted to the sustainment of the ecosphere, thus we enjoy the high-speed rail trip through the Sierra foothills, and we cheer when Ecotopians legally smoke marijuana. It could be said; therefore, that while our hearts yearn for Ecotopia, our minds realize its impossibility.

6. Add apostrophes for contractions and possessive case.

Check all apostrophes and suspect all nouns ending in -s. Use the methods outlined in Chapter 7 to get you started, and always get into the habit of preparing yourself for apostrophes and possessive situations. Check for the following common errors:

1. Are the apostrophes used in possessive situations or with contractions? These are the two most common uses for the apostrophe.
2. Have the apostrophes been used with plural nouns instead of possessive nouns? If so, get rid of them.
3. Are the apostrophes placed correctly with respect to singular or plural nouns? Remember that singular nouns get **'s** while plural nouns that end in S get **s'**. Irregular plural nouns often get the **'s**, but this depends on the situation.

See Figure 12–3 for a flowchart which details use of apostrophes.

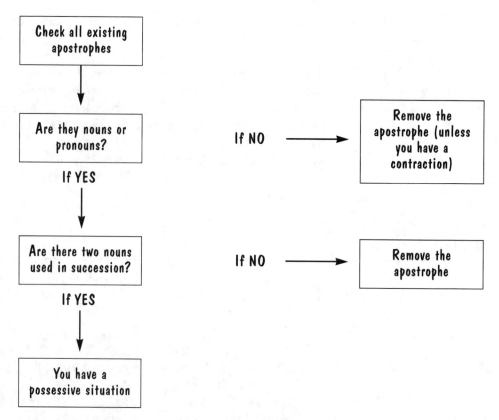

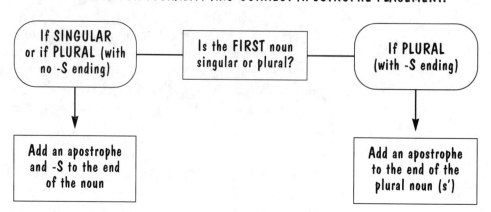

Figure 12–3 Apostrophe usage flowchart.

PRACTICE

Proofread the following paragraphs for errors with apostrophes. Look closely for contractions or possessive situations, and try to distinguish plural nouns, present tense verbs, and other -s ending words from possessive case situations.

Today's world is simply too fast paced. The pressure's of work, family and money are almost more than the average person can handle; thus, it is not difficult to understand why some people simple go over the edge and do something horrible. We have seen many such case's of a persons despair erupting in violence. In just the last few years alone, troubled individuals have taken to shooting fellow employees, neighbors, etc. What Americans must realize, however, is that it isn't just the people who have the problems, but society as a whole.

7. Pluralize nouns correctly

Always check your drafts for the correct usage of plural nouns. Most nouns simply take an -s or -es ending, but if you are not sure, use your dictionary and look the word up. DO NOT GET LAZY! This is just as important as any other aspect of either writing or proofreading. Now check out the paragraphs below. Edit them for errors with plural noun forms. Use a dictionary to help you.

Sad as it may seem, not everyone in this country is covered by a medical care plan. Many companys simply are unable to afford the steep costs of health coverage, so their employees must do without (or pay for it on their own). Many studys have been done to try to solve the problem, but even when our president proposes an idea, he is sharply criticized. We have millions of men, woman, and children in this country who must do without, so I feel that all of these damned attornies who love to blast the president ought to get together and work this plan out. I think it will be a good one.

8. Build comprehension with spelling and vocabulary.

One of the most glaring errors in writing is the simple misspelling. Nothing detracts more from an otherwise impressive piece of work than a careless spelling error. Get to know some words, and more importantly, get to know the words that you always misspell. Look for patterns in spelling, and memorize some of the more common spelling rules ("I before e, except after c" and so on). Above all else, however, always have a dictionary close at hand, both when you write and when you are proofreading. We cannot emphasize this enough! Get into the habit! If you are uncertain, look that word up, and the next time you come to it, you'll undoubtedly remember how to spell it.

When you proofread, look for longer, unfamiliar words. Often we misspell words that we do not use very often; moreover, some of the most frequently misspelled words tend to be longer.

And finally, be sure to underline and define any **vocabulary words** that you are unsure of. If you fail to learn a new word when the opportunity arises, you will be left with a boring, simple command of English for the rest of your life. We always recommend that readers have a dictionary close at hand when reading, so that you can just quickly look up any unfamiliar words. Challenge yourself to expand your vocabulary, and soon you will realize that you can read more words more quickly.

Here is some practice in misspellings:

No one knows much about the decietfulness of the U.S. government, but many cases of political dishonesty have been documented in the last decade alone. The affect that these crimes has had on the moral of our country is incalculable, but when you can no longer trust your elected officials, then who can you trust? When a president (such as Reagan or Bush) makes a conscience desicion to cheat his constituents, then we have a serious problem on our hands. We must elimanate this phenomenon of our society!

PROOFREADING CHECKLIST

Edit out (or beware of) the following:

1. comma splice ___

2. run-on sentence ___

3. sentence fragment ___

4. omitted commas ____

5. unnecessary commas ___

6. misuse of punctuation ___

7. misuse of apostrophes/plurals ___

8. misspellings ___

9. incorrect or mixed verb tenses ___

10. disagreement between subjects and verbs ___

Proofread the following paragraphs for errors in all aspects of style, usage, and mechanics. Pay very close attention to all of the things you have studied thus far in this chapter.

Whole language is an interesting approach to the teaching of English. Whole language is not necessarily a new approach, the basic concept has long been accepted by teachers. The difference; however, is that it simply is'nt used as often as it should be. The most interesting thing about whole language is that it makes sense because it involves all aspects of language, including reading, grammar, vocabulary, and writing.

Reading is certainly very important the more a person reads the more familiar he or she will become with what good prose looks like on the printed page. Reading on a regular basis it makes us aware of what paragraphs look like and it helps us to understand the way sentences work together. When a person does a lot of reading he or she is almost always a better writer. Reading has shown to improve writing but for some reason todays students are still reading less than they should.

Since vocabulary and grammar are the building blocks of language they should be included in the whole language program. We believe; however, that these two elements of language must be taught in the context of a writing situation it is the writing, the essential form of communication, that must be perfected. It is not helpful to remember a bunch of rules unless they have some kind of practical application. This would be like a baseball coach having his player's memorize the rule book and then except them to be ready for the major leagues.

Once a student has been exposed to reading, grammer, and vocabulary then they control a number of tools with which to build sentences, paragraphs, and entire essays. I like to have students' write in class so that I may view the writing process and intervene before the students writing has a chance to go astray. This emphasis on "process" rather than "finished product" is what distinguishes a writing workshop and whole language situation from other programs. The writing workshop which is lauded by English teachers nationwide, was an important step in creating a stress free environment for the actual business of writing.

Appendix

STYLE, USAGE, AND MORE

DOCUMENTATION AND FORMAT

The Modern Language Association (MLA) has devised a format and system of documentation for writers of research papers. This system of citation is used by colleges across the country and recommends that citation be made in the text rather than in footnotes or endnotes. If your instructor prefers footnotes or endnotes, follow his or her instructions.

The MLA's in-text citations are made in two ways: signal phrases, which include the page number at the end of the phrase, and parenthetical references.

Signal Phrases

Writers use transitional or signal phrases to introduce works cited in their essays. Here is an example:

> According to Franklin Smith in his book *Music By Musicians*, the influence of corporate America has "changed the way we create music" (32).

The signal phrase—"According to Franklin Smith"—provides the author's name and the parenthetical citation gives the page number where the quotation can be found. By looking up the author's name in the list of works cited, the reader can find complete information about the work's title, the publisher, and place and date of publication.

Parenthetical Citations

If there is no signal phrase and the author's name is not mentioned, then the author's last name must appear in the parenthetical citation along with the page number.

> Since music has become a business, musicians create music differently, conforming to certain markets (Smith 32).

LIST OF WORKS CITED

Whether you use a signal phrase and parenthetical citation or just a parenthetical citation, the reader must be able to find the publication you have referred to in your list of works cited. This list appears at the end of your essay. Discussed here are the ways of listing your works cited for books and magazines.

Basic Book Format

If you are using books to obtain your information, there are three basic components to the entries in your works cited section. Each unit of information is followed by a period. These three components in the order they appear are (1) the author's name, last name first; (2) the title and subtitle, underlined; and (3) the place of publication, the publisher, and the date.

> Smith, Franklin. Music by Musicians: The Struggle Between Art and Economics. Stanford: Stalsio UP, 1994.

The above information can be found on the title page and copyright pages of the book, not from the outside cover. If you have two or three authors list them in the order in which they are presented on the title page. Reverse the name of the first author only.

> Smith, Franklin and Sandra Rivera. American Popular Music: 1900–1950. Berkeley: Rocup, 1993.

Use commas to separate the names of three authors.

> Smith, Franklin, Sandra Rivera, and Phat Nguyen. The Music of Vietnam and America. Hayward: J and M, 1990.

If you have more than three authors list only the first author followed by "et al." (Latin for others).

> Smith, Franklin, et al. <u>The Death of Musical Creativity</u>: <u>Myth or Reality</u>? New York: Zappa UP, 1992.

Notice when information carries over from each entry, the information is indented five spaces. This allows a reader to locate names of authors more easily.

Basic Periodical Format

When using an article that appears in a monthly magazine, you include the month and year and the page numbers on which the article appears. Underline the title of the magazine and set the title of the article in quotation marks.

> Twain, Susan. "Current Advances in Electronics." <u>Science and Technology</u>: Feb. 7, 1993: 27–52.

If the page numbers are not consecutive, write "27+". Abbreviate the names of all the months except May, June, and July.
When you cite a weekly magazine handle the entry the same as you would a monthly magazine, only include the exact date of the issue before the month.

> Regis, Tyrone. "Technology and The Working Class." <u>Techno 23</u>: June, 1994: 15+.

While you may have other sources you use, the basic format for the list of works cited section remains the same. This information is important because it allows your reader to verify the information and leads them directly to material they might enjoy reading on the topic at hand.

Essay Format

The MLA had also devised a basic format standard used by writers of all types of essays. The format given here does not require a title page (save a tree).

One inch from the top of your paper should appear your name, your professor's name, the course title, and the date. Remember to number all pages in the upper right right hand corner, including the first page. You may also write the first four letters of your last name here, so that if your reader, God forbid, loses any of the pages of your essay, a loosed page can be immediately identified and returned to its proper place. Think of this as insurance.

Double space between every line, including the title and text. Do not use justification on the right side of your essay as you will need to space twice after each period. Type or word process all your essays on

8 1/2" by 11" paper. The following is an example of MLA format for the first and second page of a correctly formatted essay.

Floyd 1

Pink Floyd

Professor Tunes

Music 6001

8–3–94

The Business of Music

Perhaps the first sounds of music were cavemen and cave-women banging rocks and sticks together. It is unlikely another caveperson was standing by listening to hear if the song was a hit. Things have changed. According to Franklin Smith in his book <u>Music By Musicians</u>, the influence of corporate America has "changed the way we create music" (32).

Floyd 2

As it turns out, the influence of marketing on music has greatly distorted the way musicians have approached music ever since the days when the Catholic church contracted classical com-posers.

SOME SIMPLE RULES FOR USAGE

Here are a few rules that will help you remember when and in what sit-uations to use certain aspects of our language.

Apostrophes

An apostrophe is used to show that a noun is possessive. A possessive noun indicates ownership.

Franklin's car.   Ruth's house.

In the above examples Frank owns the car and Ruth owns the house. Sometimes it is difficult to determine what the noun is owning.

> the house's paint job.   the car's windshield.

If you are confused about whether or not the noun is possessive, try turning the possessive phrase into a prepositional phrase starting with of.

> the paint job of the house.   the windshield of the car.

You add -s to the end of the noun when the noun does not end with -s as in the examples above.

If a common noun is plural, you only need to add the apostrophe.

> All the trucks' wheels were aligned.
>
> The players' salaries are too high.

When a proper noun, however, ends in an -s, you must add the -'s except when pronunciation is a problem.

> The Jones's dog. Charles's glasses.

If you wish to show joint possession, use -'s with the last noun.

> Jeff and Joanne's new house looks great.

If a noun is compound use -'s (or -s') at the end of the construction.

> My mother-in-law's car was stolen.

You can also use apostrophes to mark omissions in contractions and numbers.

> Jimmy can't hit the ball. He graduated in '80.

Capitalization

Besides the following rules, any good dictionary will tell you when to capitalize letters.

1. Capitalize all proper nouns but not common nouns.

Spot	a dog
Mary	a girl
San Francisco	a city

2. The names of languages, the months, holidays, and days of the week are capitalized.
3. Capitalize the first word of every sentence; the first word of a quoted sentence unless it is part of another sentence; and the first, last, and all major words in titles of books, short stories, poems, songs, and articles.
4. Use capitalization for abbreviations of organizations, agencies, and corporations.

Noun Plurals

1. Pronouns: Subjective and Objective

Subjective Pronouns

Singular	Plural
I	we
you	you
she/he/it	they

Subjective pronouns are used as subjects of sentences and as subject complements.

> He words hard all day.
>
> She was happy because her boyfriend and she got engaged.
>
> The writer of the book was he.

Don't be misled when using subjective pronouns as subject complements. In speech we frequently incorrectly use objective pronouns instead.

Objective Pronouns

Singular	**Plural**
me	us
you	you
him, her, it	them

Objective pronouns are used as direct objects, indirect objects, and objects of the preposition.

> He hit me.
>
> I gave him a black eye.
>
> Between you and me, they both are crazy.

Be careful again not to let your ear mislead you. Ask your instructor for help if you are unsure.

2. Compound Subjects, Objects, and Verbs
    The meaning of things becomes compounded when coordination is used. Earlier you studied how to make compound sentences using the FAN-BOYS. The same principles apply to subjects, objects, and verbs.

> John and I ate lunch.
>
> She and her friend flew to Hawaii.
>
> Your mother or I will pick you up.

> He gave me a pencil and paper.
>
> You can eat the cake and the ice cream.
>
> He did not want the car nor the motorcycle.

> I run and walk every day.
>
> She studied hard and passed the test.
>
> They bought a lottery ticket but did not win.

Notice how the coordinating conjunction in the sentences above join the subjects, objects, and verbs so that one sentence can be written instead of two.

General Punctuation

1. Colons
   Use colons after independent clauses for lists and quotations:

   > There are three ingredients for good study skills: time management, a quiet place, and self discipline.

   > My brother is always espousing his belief: "Electronics is the most important field of study today."

2. Exclamation Point
   The exclamation point is used to show extreme emotion or emphasis. Interjections are often followed by exclamation points.

   > Wow! I won a million dollars.

   > Money is falling from the sky!

   Do not use more than one exclamation point at the end of a sentence.

3. Question Mark
   Always use a question mark after a direct question.

   > Did you go to the dance?

   Polite requests also need question marks.

   > Please give me a copy of your book?

   Indirect questions do not need question marks.

   > She asked him if he would marry her.

Subject/Verb Agreement

In present tense, verbs must agree with their subjects in number and person. For third person singular use an -s ending. Consider the chart below.

	Singular	**Plural**
First Person	I walk	we walk
Second Person	you walk	you walk
Third Person	he/she/it walks	they walk

Compound subjects are treated as plural

> He and I walk.

Most indefinite pronouns and collective nouns are treated as singular.

> Each has a responsibility to his or her teammate.
>
> The jury is deliberating.

If the subject is plural, then the verb must also be plural.

> Tests are always difficult.
>
> A voltmeter and a screwdriver are required equipment for a technician.

INDEX

interrogative, 16
objective, 191
personal, 15
plural, 17, 190-91
possessive, 15
reflexive, 17
relative, 16
subjective, 190
as subjects of sentences, 14
Proofreading, 174-84
for apostrophe usage, 179-81
checklist, 183
for comma usage, 177-78
for coordination of conjunctive adverbs
and semicolons, 179
importance of, 174
for pluralized nouns, 181
for sentence structure, 176-77
for spelling and vocabulary, 181-82
validity of response, checking, 175
for verb choice, 175-76
Proper nouns, 15, 190
Protagonist, 172
Punctuation, 133-45, 192
colons, 143, 192
dash, 139-40
exclamation point, 192
parentheses, 140
question marks, 192
quotation marks, 140-45, 187
run-on sentences lacking, 56-57
semicolon, 53, 133-38, 179
as street signs of language, 133

Question marks, 192
Questions
asking, 6
direct, question mark after, 192
indirect, 192
Quotation marks, 140-45
for direct quotations, 141-42
for quotations within quotations, 142-43
quoting longer passages, 143
smooth transitions with, 143-45
for titles of short works, 140-41, 187
Quotations
colons after independent clauses for, 192
MLA citation format, 185-86

Radio episodes, quotation marks denoting titles of, 140
Raup, Dave, 149
Reader participation, 170
Reading
active, 169-71
of literature, 171-74
for characterization, 171, 172
for plot, 171-72
for point of view, 172-73
for setting, 173
for tone, 173-74
Reason in persuasive writing, 149
Reflexive pronouns, 17
Relative pronouns, 16

Relevant senses, appealing to, 31-32
Researching, 2
Revision, 7, 10
Rising action, 171, 172
Romero, Blanca E., 156
Roth, Bobby, 129
Run-on sentences, 56-57
proofreading for, 176

Salinger, J.D., 172
Secondary causes, 118
Second draft, 7
Second person, subject/verb agreement in, 193
Second person point of view, 173
Semicolon, 133-38
with conjunctive adverbs, 134-38, 179
for sentence construction, 133-34
separation of independent clauses with, 55, 134
Senses, appealing to, 29-33
Sentence
capitalization in, 190
complex, 53
compound, 53, 85
compound-complex, 53
concluding, 110-11
parts of, 52-53
simple, 53
subjects of, 14
syntax, 112
topic, 109-10, 111
transition between paragraphs with, 111
Sentence construction, semicolon for, 133-34
Sentence fragment, 53, 54
proofreading for, 176
Sentence structure, 51-59
errors of, 53-57
comma splice, 55-56, 176, 177
run-on or fused sentence, 56-57, 176
sentence fragment, 53, 54, 176
exercises on, 58-59
parts of sentence, 52-53
proofreading for, 176-77
reasons to learn about, 51
Sepkoski, Jack, 149
Series, comma between three or more items in, 178
Setting, 173
Short stories, quotation marks denoting titles of, 140
Sight, images appealing to, 30
Signal phrases, 185-86
Similarities, comparison/contrast to show, 93
Simile, use of, 32-33
Simple past tense, 175
Simple present tense, 175
Simple sentence, 53
Simple verb tenses, 20
Since, 87
Single quotes, 142-43
So, 55, 84-85
Speech, parts of. *See* Parts of speech